THE OCEANUS AT THE DOCK IN CHARLESTON.

THE TRIP

OF THE

STEAMER OCEANUS

TO

Fort Sumter and Charleston, S. C.

Comprising the Incidents of the Excursion, the Appearance, at that time, of the City, and the entire Programme of Exercises at the Re-raising of the Flag over the Ruins of

FORT SUMTER,

APRIL 14th, 1865.

BY A COMMITTEE APPOINTED BY THE PASSENGERS OF THE OCEANUS.

BROOKLYN:
"THE UNION" STEAM PRINTING HOUSE, 10 FRONT STREET.

1865.

INTRODUCTORY NOTE.

The preparation of this book, whatever may be its reception by those to whom it is dedicated, has been a labor of love. Unsought, and almost under protest, the work was undertaken, at the unanimous request of the passengers of the "Oceanus." It was an addition to stated professional duties, which the committee appointed were exceedingly reluctant to accept. But, once begun, it brought its reward continually, in the joy of living over again minutely, every scene which made the excursion to Charleston the most memorable as to object, enjoyment and inspiration, which our national history has ever made possible.

The work effects no faultlessness. In the brief space during which it was composed, there was little opportunity for elaboration. It professes to be, not a treatise upon national affairs, nor yet a discussion of principles, but a current, unimaginative, and therefore we trust, a perfectly truthful narration of scenes and incidents, from the hour the "Oceanus" left the wharf, until she brought us there again. The writers describe not only what was seen and enjoyed by themselves, but by hundreds of others, who are asked to bear witness to the faithfulness of these records.

The delay in issuing the memorial, has arisen from the necessary occupation of time in the mechanical execution. But if any have indulged impatience, we confidently believe that they will be amply repaid by the style of typography, illustration and general finish, in which the work is presented.

The committee, to whom the preparation of the volume was entrusted, would gratefully acknowledge the kindly assistance, through communicated incidents, gleanings from the press, notices of relics, and manifestations of deep interest in the work, rendered by many of their fellow-voyagers.

To Mr. E. Anthony, of the firm "E. & H. T. Anthony," No. 501 Broadway, New York, who had an artist in the field, and who kindly permitted his copy-righted views to be used for illustration, the committee of publication would tender their hearty thanks, in the name of the "Sumter Club."

In conclusion, they would state that this book is not an avant-courier. Authorship was as far from their intention as desire. An edition, covering but few more copies than those actually subscribed for by the passengers of the "Oceanus," is all that will be issued. The public may therefore rest assured, that it will then be out of print, and in this case, the Scriptural assertion, "of making *many* books there is no end," will have a positive exception.

If, in the perusal of these pages, those who visited the ruined city and the storied Fort, shall experience any satisfaction; if in coming years, it shall delight any one to remember the historic excursion, the better by these simple records; if any impulse shall be given to the sacred cause of loyalty to our common country, the whole desire of those who now commit them to the public view, will be abundantly answered.

To the Sumter Club,

Extemporized in origin: unexampled in occasion: abounding with the representatives of pulpit, press, forum, and counting-room: graced with feminine beauty and culture: a synonym for patriotic devotion to

"THE FLAG OF OUR UNION,"

the anniversary of whose resurrection in Charleston Harbor it is henceforth to celebrate with

"FEAST OF REASON, AND FLOW OF LOYAL SOUL,"

this volume is primarily and cordially

DEDICATED.

THE TRIP OF THE OCEANUS

TO

Fort Sumter and Charleston, South Carolina.

CHAPTER I.

When the welcome intelligence reached the North that Charleston was occupied by the victorious legions of Gen. Sherman, the expectation was universal that a day would be appointed for the formal raising of the United States flag over the ruins of Fort Sumter.

That expectation, our President did not disappoint. With that unerring discernment of appropriate times and seasons, for which he was ever remarkable, he named the fourteenth of April, the fourth anniversary of the surrender, and the lowering of the banner for a four years' banishment. From the first appearance of this proclamation, it was felt that the occasion would be one around which national and historic interest would gather. Upon that day, every loyal son of the United States would exult, and give praise to God; every traitor or sympathizer with treason, if not too hardened, would blush for the temerity and wickedness which attempted dishonor to the nation's standard; every well-wisher to the American Republic, in foreign lands, would sing in his heart a glad "*Te Deum.*"

It was known that a steamer, officially commissioned, would convey to the Fort all those who were to take active part in the exercises, together with a few more favored individuals; but what should they do, who were not within that charmed circle, the "*ignobile vulgus,*" who were not so happy as Government patronage, just at this time, would have made them? Fortunately, a few gentlemen, to whom all the passengers of the Oceanus, upon that ever-memorable excursion, will always be grateful, conceived and executed a plan to afford this pleasure to a goodly number of their fellow-citizens.

These gentlemen were Messrs. Stephen M. Griswold and Edwin A. Studwell, of Brooklyn, who subsequently associated with themselves Mr. Edward Cary, Editor of *The Union*, whose services were confined, however, to issuing the tickets and receiving the money at the office of that paper. In pursuance of a plan arranged by these gentlemen, the steamer "Oceanus" was chartered of the Neptune Steamship Company, G. S. Howland, President, for nine days, for which time she was turned over to the Committee for a trip to Charleston, and such other points as the passengers should decide to visit. Originally, the plan of the trip embraced not only Charleston Harbor and Fort Sumter, but Hilton Head, Fort Fisher, Fortress Monroe, Norfolk, Portsmouth, and possibly City Point, to which—when we heard of the fall of the Rebel capital—Richmond, also, was conditionally added. The expenses of the trip were divided among the passengers equally, so that $100 paid for berth and meals for the round trip.

The first announcement of the proposed excursion was made in *The Union* of March 30th, in a very modest and succinct manner; the statement was repeated on the following day, and also made from Mr. Beecher's pulpit on Sunday. The result was a rush for tickets, beginning on the 31st, and increasing to such an extent that on Monday, the 3d of April, the Committee enlarged the number of passengers from one hundred and fifty, as originally determined, to one hundred and eighty. The scenes in the office of *The Union* were extremely amusing, resulting from the earnestness of the applicants, their nervous anxiety each to secure the best accommodations possible, and from the hearty good humor with which all treated each other. The increase in the number of passengers wholly failed to satisfy the demand; twice as many would have eagerly taken the opportunity to go, if possible, and another party was projected, which was abandoned only because no other suitable steamer could be obtained.

Finally, on the eighth of April, it was duly announced

that all the preparations were completed. The contract* for the boat had been duly signed, the tickets disposed of, passes obtained for the passengers individually, and a very liberal general permit, direct from the War Department, for the vessel—the latter largely through the kind offices of Mr. H. C. Bowen, of the *Independent;* the provender had been stored, the vessel put in seagoing order, and Hon. Cyrus P. Smith, President of the Union Ferry Company, had kindly proffered the use of one of the largest of the East River ferry-boats to transfer the passengers from the foot of Montague Street to the dock of the Oceanus, at the foot of Robinson Street, on the North River, whence the excursionists were to start at noon, precisely, of the 10th.

On the morning of the 10th, at half-past ten, the Fulton Ferry boat Peconic started with her joyous company, which was duly transferred to the Oceanus. The scenes at the wharf of the steamer were characteristic: the passengers coming on board in good time and cheerily, while many were still awaiting a possible vacancy. The only addition to the company was Col. Howard, of the 128th Colored Regiment, who was eager to reach his command at Charleston, having just come from Sherman's triumphant army at Savannah, where he had been attached to the staff of his brother, Gen. Howard. The time for departure having come, the crowd upon the wharf gathered to bid us God-speed.

And a God-speed we had—possibly barring the speed—

* See Appendix.

but with good cheer, good nature, faithful seas, grand music, glowing patriotism, congenial company, hearts over-brimming with joy—save the last Dark Day—and pre-eminent Divine favor, from the hour that we waved our adieus, till again we touched the wharf at the foot of Robinson Street — all of which we will proceed to narrate with as much faithfulness as possible in the next and succeeding chapters.

CHAPTER II.

At 10 minutes past 12 o'clock M., April 10th, the screw of the good steamer Oceanus began its recalcitration, slowly pushing its precious and happy freight out upon the bosom of the river. Cheer upon cheer broke forth from the crowd gathered upon the wharf, responded to by the passengers filling every available standing place upon the vessel's landward side; hats and handkerchiefs were waved in the air, and parting messages exchanged, until the shouting and signals became futile by the increasing distance. It was evident that we had left hundreds of envious and yet congratulatory hearts behind. *We* bore our enjoyment and honors meekly.

The day was in unhappy mood. All the morning the skies had lowered. A fine, filtering mist had only slightly dampened our ardor. Now the rain increased, and a tenuous fog thickened gradually over the surface of the bay. It was not an auspicious inauguration of our voyage, but the doubting were assured by the hopeful, who quoted the venerable and philosophic maxim "A bad beginning makes a good ending."

In the smooth waters of the harbor, we were pluming

ourselves upon the delightful steadiness of the steamer. The inexperienced were sure that the discomforts of a sea voyage, must have been greatly overstated. Now we pass Governor's Island, and the familiar landmarks in our own enterprising City; we leave upon our left, Fort Lafayette, that boarding place of sundry treason-enacting individuals, and upon our right, the fortifications and heights of Staten Island; now we point out the low sandy waste of Coney Island, and descry in the misty distance the light-house of Sandy Hook. It is the opinion of the writer that somewhere near this locality the hitherto staid steamer began to lose its reputation for steadiness, and certain passengers, whose temperance and sobriety is proverbial, to exhibit strange symptoms of inebriety. Upon this point, however, owing to temporary aberration of his own intellect, he would prefer not to be considered authority. Yet he has sufficient distinctness of memory to recall a peculiarly gyratory motion among the passengers, as they attempted to navigate the cabin, the clutching here and there of an outsider at the gunwale, and occasional visages of more than ordinary pallor. He remembers one gentleman of portly carriage and still happy face, standing near the cabin entrance with his friends, who, upon a sudden roll of the vessel, was caught just behind the knees by an opportune chair, and, as he was tilted over backward into its cushioned receptacle, remarked somewhat drily, "I believe I'll sit down." The situation, which had been in a good degree comical, was now becoming more serious, when suddenly—*rub*—*thump*—*stop*—and we were aground. We had struck the sand-spit, and all the tempest of the screw only sufficed to beat the shallow waters into unavailing foam at the stern. We hailed our supposed deliverer in a puffing, spitting steam-tug, just in the offing, but which, upon being lashed to the great hulk of the Oceanus, appeared like an ant tugging at a kernel of corn, and was about as efficient. Signal was given for a pilot-boat, which soon came bearing down before the breeze, and when within fifty yards, dropped a row-boat astern, containing a pilot, and two oarsmen. Soon an order comes for the gentlemen to go forward, as the vessel is aground aft. We all go out upon the forward deck, and stand with commendable patience in the sifting rain. The effect becomes speedily apparent, for, depressed at the bow by such a weight of corporeal and mental ballast, the ship swings clear of the sand, and we discover by the buoys that we are drifting free. A few querulous individuals undertake to chaffer with the old salt, who stands with arms akimbo upon the window casement of the pilot-house. They soon learn that the experience of twenty years at sea not only perfects the nautical science, but sharpens the wits of a New York Harbor pilot.

"Can't you take us out this afternoon?" asks an impatient passenger.

"I reckon I can, if you say so," responds the son of Neptune; "but you'd better lay *here* to-night."

"Why so?"

"You gentlemen want to go to Charleston, don't you?"

"Of course"—from a dozen voices.

"Wall, you'd better lay here then to-night, for it's goin' to be a werry dirty, nasty night outside."

Meanwhile, the Committee are holding a conference with the captain, and returning, submit the question to the vote of the passengers, which, by a very large majority, is decided in favor of remaining for clearer weather, until morning if necessary; accordingly, while a few of the opposition are warmly debating the possibilities of danger and too long delay, lest we might miss the celebration of the coming Friday, with a rush and noise like small thunder down goes the anchor, and we lie as motionless in the shallow waters at Sandy Hook as if moored at the wharf at the foot of Robinson St. The temporarily sea-sick reäppear. The cabins are filled with groups of ladies and gentlemen joyously discussing the morning news of the surrender of Lee, the prospects of the excursion, and the sensible conclusion to wait for brighter skies; or, disposed in various attitudes, and with nondescript pens and pencils, and extemporized bits of letter paper, writing a few words to home friends, jocularly dating their missives, "*On* Sandy Hook." A well-known fellow-citizen of the happiest countenance acts as collecter of these epistles, and is the mail-carrier to the pilot.

The Chairman of the Committee summons the passengers to the deck below, and explains to them the arrangements for the trip, the sea-worthiness of the vessel, the capacity and variety of the larder, and answers the queries of the inquisitive with satisfactory minuteness and good nature.

Nothing was left us now but to kill time in the most entertaining and profitable manner possible; and it was to the quick intelligence of a lady that we were indebted for a patriotic meeting in the evening, which was the jubilant key-note for all its successors; a series of meetings, whose enjoyableness in all the elements of patriotic fervor and eloquence, pathos, breadth, wit, and humor, is seldom equaled.

The meeting of Monday evening was organized by the appointment of Hon. Cyrus P. Smith, President; Hon. Edward A. Lambert, Joshua Leavitt, D. D., Henry C. Bowen, Hon. A. M. Wood, and S. M. Griswold, Vice-Presidents, Hon. George Hall and Mr. E. A. Studwell, Secretaries. Mr. Wm. B. Bradbury kindly consented to act as Director-General of music, the piano being generously furnished for the trip by Messrs. Sawyer & Thompson.

The most humorous introduction was given to the exercises by the facetious proposition to sing, in beginning, "We are out on the ocean sailing"—the most perfect burlesque upon our situation, fast at the end of an anchor chain, and as motionless as the hills of Nevisink. When the explosion of laughter which greeted this announcement had subsided, the familiar Sabbath-school glee was sung with a will. Peculiarly suggestive to many seemed the last three lines:

"When we all are safely landed
Over on that golden shore,
We *will walk about the city,*" etc., etc.

Rev. Theo. L. Cuyler was called upon to state the object of the meeting. For half an hour he stated it with anecdote and illustration, reminiscence and appeal, in a strain of fervid, patriotic eloquence, and resumed his seat amidst a storm of applause. His speech was a fitting preparation for the soul-stirring song, "Rally round the flag, boys!" which followed at his request. We may remark, in passing, that throughout the entire excursion, the unusual amount of excellent musical as well as speaking talent was brought into daily requisition.

The second speaker of the evening was Rev. O. B. Frothingham, whose well-considered, earnest, and timely address was listened to with very marked attention.

Rev. H. M. Gallaher, of the Nassau Street Baptist Church, a stranger to many of the party at the outset, was next introduced, and for nearly an hour kept the company in a tumult of laughter and applause by his side-splitting stories, his racy narrations, his broad comedy, his glowing eulogies of his adopted country — he is an Irishman — and his brilliant climaxes. He was no longer a stranger to the passengers of the Oceanus.

Mr. Bradbury's spirited national glee, "Victory at last," which all the musical on board seemed to catch as by intuition, was then sung with a vociferous effect, which might almost have been heard on shore. This song became one of the indispensable spiceries of every occasion, and, by the kind permission of its author, is to be found, with the music, in the appendix.

A brief address was made by Rev. J. Clement French, followed by Col. Howard, previously mentioned. The Colonel's address was replete with practical common sense, and with frank and cordial acknowledgment of the services of the privates, such as might have been expected from a true soldier, whose best record is to be found in his deeds.

After the grand old Doxology, "Praise God from whom all blessings flow," the meeting adjourned, subject to the call of the President.

And it was high time, for, during the speeches of the last two gentlemen, the sounds of hurrying feet upon the decks had been heard; the welcome news had been whispered through the company that we were weighing anchor, and were about to proceed on our way; the now familiar roll of the ship began again to be experienced; the speakers were steadying themselves against the table and iron braces of the cabin, and a very few of the most sensitive had quietly withdrawn to their state-rooms. Going forth to the bow, we found that the steamer had already left the lights of Sandy Hook far in the distance, the dull clouds were opening in rifts, through which the friendly moon smiled promises of a fairer sky; the pilot was gone, and we were fairly at sea.

Despite the inspiriting effects of these pleasant omens, the duty of an honest historian compels us to state that certain stalwart gentlemen, with an excess of self-denial, gave whatsoever they had laid by at the supper-table to the fishes of the sea. The general impression seemed to prevail that it was high time for all honest and patriotic individuals to be in their berths. Further than this, concerning Monday night, your deponent saith not.

To attempt a description of the scenes on board our vessel throughout Tuesday, Wednesday, and Thursday morning for you indeed, might be amusing, but for us, "it is not convenient." A strange oblivion concerning those hours settles upon our memory. We remember hearing the strains of Helmsmuller's Band contending with the creaking of the rolling ship, and the dashing of the waves; an occasional flourish by some fair hand upon the piano, supplemented by a distressed sound in the after cabin; the voice of Helon Johnson, the colored waiter, singing in the adjoining state-room the tantalizing ditty,

"Rocked in the cradle of the deep,
I lay me down in peace to sleep,"

—the rich sweetness of whose tones only enhanced the impertinent mockery; the unsteady tread of the exempt, as they shambled past our door; the untouched bowls of soup; the prescriptions without number of sea-water, brandy, mustard, lemon-juice, ice-cream, salt pork, *et id omne genus;* the glimpses we caught through the crack of the door of serried rows of mattresses in the cabins, each bearing a pale-faced, despairing female, whose head was in painful proximity to a little green, semi-lunar basin of tin, with chambermaids hurrying to and fro, themselves worn down by constant service; the brave resistance to sea-sickness by our room-mate, who had weathered the storms of Lake Erie and Michigan, until the heavy sea of Thursday morning obliged him to succumb; how he rushed into the state-room where we were writhing in superlative wretchedness, divested himself, in a twinkling, of his outer and nether integuments, plunged into his berth with the expressive declaration, "Whew! I'm as dizzy as a bat," until we of the lower berth writhed again with irrepressible laughter—these few distinct recollections come floating through the vagueness which gathers over those darksome days, and may serve as hints for those who desire to treasure up the more ludicrous incidents of the voyage.

But the meetings went on, with diminished numbers, it is true, but with no abatement of interest. On Tuesday evening, Edward A. Lambert, Esq., presided. We were told that the Rev. A. P. Putnam made the opening address, fully equaling the occasion in impressiveness and power; that the Rev. J. L. Corning spoke pointedly and pleasantly; that Charlton T. Lewis, Esq., of New York, delighted the audience with the clearness and force of his thought, and the graceful finish of his rhetoric; that Rev. H. M. Gallaher again scintillated with increasing popularity; and Rev. Dr. Leavitt gave weight and dignity to the occasion by his narrations of personal experience, and forceful utterances of practical truth, while music and applause and laughter filled up all the interstices of the hastily-fleeting hours.

We were indebted, on each of these occasions, to Miss Phœbe B. Merritt and Miss Mary Bowen for some excellent piano solos.

Wednesday passed with little of special interest. The sea was calmer. Cape Hatteras had been cleared without inconvenience additional. We were experiencing a marked modification of temperature. State-rooms became uncomfortably close. It was said that the sea outrivaled the sky in the depth and infinity of blue; that a school of porpoises rolled their black backs above the waves in merry gambols around the steamer, and that those who had "oil on the brain" looked with stoical indifference upon a whale. It was also averred that the culinary and dietetic arrangements were becoming more and more satisfactory, and that the number gathered about the board was upon the increase.

A third meeting was held in the evening, presided over by Hon. A. M. Wood, of Brooklyn.

The first speaker upon this occasion was Mr. A. M. Powell, a correspondent of the *Tribune.* His address was thoughtful, earnest, radical, and convincing.

Col. Howard, Hon. Edgar Ketchum, Dr. J. Allen, Revs. T. L. Cuyler and H. M. Gallaher, with others, continued the interest of our former gatherings. At the close, several of the colored waiters, whose choruses upon the lower decks had attracted much attention, were invited to sing for our company. Coming modestly into so august a presence, they rendered the "John Brown" song with peculiarly fine effect.

Throughout the afternoon of Wednesday, and part of the night, we were enveloped in an impenetrable fog. But the morning of Thursday was clear and beautiful, with no other motion for our vessel than that imparted by the long roll of the sea. But this was now excessive. The steamer, being a propellor, had nothing with which to overcome the trough of the sea, in which we were fearfully rocking. She would make from four to six heavy lurches, then, for a few seconds, all would be comparatively quiet; then as many more rolls, and all things not lashed down, including men and women, pitch across the cabin. Some of the stoutest and bravest had to show the white feather this morning. The rear cabin again became a hospital. It was thought that we must be very near Charleston. We were promised the sight of its spires by eight o'clock A. M., but we did not see them. All day long, until three o'clock, the steamer's course was laid nearly due west. How could it be that we were so far from land? At last it was ascertained that during the night we had been borne to the eastward by the Gulf stream, and this distance was now being recovered.

At length, not far from three o'clock, the joyful shout, "Land ho!" quickened the languid pulses, dissipated the *ennui*, called out of their seclusion the pallid and bilious-tinted, and crowded the deck with eager-eyed searchers, through opera-glasses, for the coveted terra-firma. The light-ship was plainly visible, upon whose side, the most clear-sighted could read the suggestive name, "Rattlesnake Shoals." Beyond could be descried the low reach of land: a dim pile, which we were assured was Fort Sumter, and still further, the spires of the once proud, but now humbled, Charleston. The arrival on board of the pilot completed our satisfaction, and the welcome he received was unfeigned.

He was a short, stout man, dressed in army blue, with which the color of his large, flat eye precisely corresponded. His face was nut-brown, from the tinting of Southern breezes. He was born and brought up in Charleston. He at once informed the captain that the bar could not be passed until high-tide, at six o'clock. Accordingly, the anchor was dropped, and we gently rocked for two hours "in the cradle of the deep." This pilot is now in Government employ. When asked if all the people of Charleston were loyal, he shrugged his shoulders, and made no reply.

One said: "We are going down to *make* you loyal."

"You won't make *me* loyal," said the old tar, "for I always *have* been."

We afterwards learned that his testimony concerning himself was true.

2

CHAPTER III.

THE scenes which greeted the passengers of the Oceanus, as we slowly steamed toward and through the harbor of Charleston, not even the most stolid and impassable will ever forget.

At precisely six o'clock, anchor was weighed. The entire company was upon the decks, with glasses ready for observation. The band took its position upon the very bow. Previous to starting from the anchorage, there had been a brief shower, giving a delicious freshness to the air, and leaving the western heavens overspread with heavy, breaking clouds of gray. Suddenly a sign appeared before us, of singular and portentous interest. The rays of the sun smote a circular opening in the murky clouds, hemming their edges with a band of light, and, just for a moment, poured down a flood of glory upon the jagged walls of Fort Sumter, and the waters of the harbor.

The pilot stood at the window, from which, besides giving his directions to the helmsman, he announced the various points of interest, as we approached and passed them.

The first object of note was a line of low earthworks

upon the left shore, upon the top of which were several soldiers, whose muskets glistened in the light. They were watching the approach of our vessel, and as we moved along, ran wildly down to the sandy beach, waving their handkerchiefs in joyous welcome. Just beyond, were two buoys, marking the spots where the Keokuk and Weehawken were sunk, the staff upon the bow of the latter being visible, to which the hand of some eager patriot had lashed a small American flag.

We would not fail to record another display in the sky, which just at this point arrested every gaze, and called forth from the entranced observers, at length, a burst of the wildest enthusiasm. It was no mere figment of the imagination, but a vision to the reality and beauty of which every passenger on the Oceanus was a delighted witness.

All at once arose a cry of admiration, as a hundred hands pointed to the spectacle. "See! the red, white, and blue! the red, white, and blue!"—for there, right before us in the western heavens, the scarlet streakings of the sunlight lay in parallel bars of amazing equidistance upon the grayish blue background of mist, intermingled here and there with white bands of the nearer clouds, the whole forming a singularly perfect picture of our beloved flag, hung out, as it seemed, by the hand of God, over the recovered city, and greeting with its celestial benison the sons and daughters of the North who were bringing the tidings of Lee's surrender, and the death of the Rebellion.

As the thought, in all its significance, suffused our souls, many an eye was moist, and hands were clasped, in the devoutness of joy.

Now, we are passing a long and low tongue of land, beyond which the bay returns backward. Upon this stands Fort Wagner, of the deepest historic interest. Here, for the first time, it was demonstrated that negroes could and would fight terribly, desperately, even to decimation. Along that narrow causeway, exposed to the murderous direct fire from the Fort, the dauntless regiment charged with the impetuosity of a tempest, to be rolled back by the torrent of shot and shell; again and again rallied and charged against fearful odds, until their Colonel, the noble and lamented Shaw, fell in his blood, the idol of his men, and the admired of all the brave.

It is not certainly known where his body sleeps. There were some of Carolinian blood, whose appreciation of heroism rose no higher than the plantation edict: "Bury him with his niggers!" Some say that his remains were scattered by the Rebels to the four winds of heaven. Others affirm that they were buried obscurely near the spot on which he fell. It is reported, also, that when it was proposed to his father to remove the dust of the heroic soldier to some other burial-place, he replied that "he wanted no better or nobler grave for his son than the very soil upon which he poured out his blood."

Next, we pass Sullivan's Island, upon the angle of

FORT SUMTER—FROM THE HARBOR.

which was the famous Cummings' Point Battery, built of railroad iron, and which rolled the cannon-shot of Sumter from its sides as though they had been peas.

Now we are approaching Fort Sumter itself, the centre of all present observation and interest. There it lies, like a vast disabled monster, crouching in sullen and conscious imbecility, in the centre of the harbor. Its parapets, once so lovely, are battered into jagged shapelessness. Its sides are deeply pock-marked and indented. Heaps of rubbish and *débris* around its base disclose the terrific ordeal through which it has passed since April, 1861. From the new flag-staff in its centre waves the Banner of the Republic, never again to be displaced by the hand of the traitor. Its port-holes are mostly closed. Rows of wicker baskets can be descried, filling up the ghastly chasms. Here and there upon the walls, a sentinel paces to and fro. Involuntarily our heads are all uncovered. A solemn silence pervades the throng, as for a moment the thought of the past four years, with their changes, passions, carnage, suffering, defeats depression, and final triumph flashes through every mind. There is but one language which can express the emotions of that moment. It is the language of thankful song. And, as by a common inspiration, our voices break forth in one grand, surging, heaven-echoed chorus:

"Praise God, from whom all blessings flow!
Praise Him, all creatures here below!
Praise Him above, ye Heavenly Host!
Praise Father, Son, and Holy Ghost!"

That allelulia is heard by the guardians of the old

ruin. In quick response, the flag is dipped, the walls bristle with armed men waving their salute; the band peals forth the "Star Spangled Banner"—fitting harmony to be rolled back upon the recreant sons of the South Carolinian who penned its measures—and we move on to other scenes. Fort Sumter! *au revoir!*

Just beyond the ruin, at the left, lies the wreck ot the famous old floating-battery, built by Beauregard, with which to take the fort. A portion of one of its sides, with four port-holes visible, still remains above the water. Near by, are the wrecks of two English blockade-runners, the smoke-stacks and bowsprit only being in sight. To the right is Fort Moultrie,—abandoned by Major Anderson and his brave followers in 1861, for the stronger defense of Fort Sumter, now in good condition, though never a fortification of superior strength. Battery Bee extends its low earth-mounds, now green with luxuriant grass, for a long distance towards the city. Fort Ripley appears in the midst of the water, a small and insignificant redoubt, built by the Rebels, with the stones taken from the streets of Charleston.

Beyond, and of more importance, rises Castle Pinckney, surrounded by a high light-house.

On either side of the harbor, the shores are crowned with groves of the pines peculiar to this country, their tops branching and interwoven, and presenting to the inexperienced, the appearance of the palmetto. This latter tree shows itself but sparsely here. We saw but one or two specimens, and these were as crooked and uninteresting as the natives whose cross-grained State they symbolize.

All these places of martial reputation were greeted as we passed, with cheers, the band meanwhile playing patriotic airs, for we saw waving above them all, the Banner of the Free.

We were now abreast of the United States vessels-of-war at anchor, the blockading vessels released from service, the captured blockade runners, the Government transports, and two monitors scarcely clearing the water's edge. To each of these we shouted the news, which was received with wild hurrahs, and the rapid dipping of the colors. A unique and beautiful sight presented itself through the thickly gathering twilight, as we steamed past the men-of-war. At a given signal, the boys in blue sprang to the shrouds, ran up like so many squirrels, walked out upon the yard-arms, filled all the rigging, and aspired even to the top-masts; then turning about, they waved their hats in exultation, and sent their ringing cheers across the water.

The monitors lie nearest the city. It is easy to understand the contempt which the Rebels felt for the first craft of this description, as commanded by the gallant Worden, it bore down upon their vast lumbering monster, the Merrimac, in the waters of Hampton Roads. Their title, bestowed at that time, was certainly graphic, "A Yankee cheese-box afloat." And yet the "cheese-box" has poured contempt upon the "wooden walls" of England, and revolutionized the naval warfare of the world.

Darkness was now settling heavily upon us. We could dimly discern the Battery, with its row of once magnificent mansions, with the marks of shells upon them. Before us lay the City, dead to all appearances. Half a dozen lights gleamed along the wharves, but these were upon our own vessels. Not the flickering of a taper was to be seen in any other part of the City. It was the very darkness of desolation. We could see the crowds gathering upon the wharves and vessels. As we drew nearer, a voice was heard faintly calling through the gloom.

"What's the news?"

One of our company, a man of stentorian lungs, putting his hands to his mouth, roared forth, the thrilling intelligence.

"Lee has surrendered, with his whole army!" Again, the voice from the shore, faintly.

"Have we got Lee!"

"Yes!" thundered the spokesman, and then from the shore, uprose such a peal of huzzas, such a wild tumult of exultation as made the night vocal. The band on board the Blackstone, which lay at the wharf, struck up the "Star Spangled Banner," to which our band responded "My Country, 'tis of Thee," then again from the shore, the "Red, White and Blue," and from the Oceanus, "Hail Columbia!" and enthusiasm indescribable reigned. As we came up to the anchorage near the wharf, we waited for a permit to enter the dock. Though Gen. Gilmore had not yet arrived from Hilton Head, an officer from one of the U. S. steamers from Savannah, having a very creditable faith in our loyalty, boldly cut red tape, and authorized our captain to swing up to the wharf.

This done, a few eager members of the party were determined to go ashore. Much confusion ensued, but at length half a dozen succeeded in their purpose, and made their way to the Charleston Hotel, where they announced the news to Gen. Wilson, and others. The wharf was covered with a motley gang of native negroes, contrabands, poor whites and rough-looking fellows, whose appearance was anything but an invitation to familiarity. The remainder of the party retired to the supper table to satisfy an appetite whetted by long delay. After supper, a meeting was called in the Ladies' Cabin. Dr. Leavitt was appointed Chairman. He said that it would be regarded by all as eminently appropriate, after so many and signal mercies, through which we had been safely brought to our destination, to recognize the goodness of Almighty God.

Rev. J. S. Corning was called upon to make a few remarks, befitting the occasion, at the conclusion of which Rev. J. Clement French was invited to offer a prayer of thanksgiving to God for his "eminent mercy to ourselves since we left New York, and his great loving kindness to our beloved country."

Pleasant speeches followed. By 10 o'clock the party which had gone ashore, returned, bringing with them flowers which they had gathered from the gardens.

Rev. Mr. Cuyler, holding up a boquet of roses and mock oranges, made it the text for one of his most effective addresses. Capt. Hunt, of Brig.-Gen. Hatch's staff, brought us the salutations of the officer commanding, and in his name tendered us the freedom of the city, with promise of conveyance, and privilege of gathering all the flowers we might desire. Gen. Hartwell, and Major Nutt, of the 155th Colored Regt., who had just returned from a ten days raid into the interior of S. C. entertained us until midnight with accounts of their adventures, and we reluctantly retired, that we might be refreshed for the visit to the city on the following morning.

CHAPTER IV.

THE morning of the ever memorable Friday, April 14th, dawned at length. It is surmised that more of the passengers of the Oceanus witnessed its rising sun than are wont to behold that matin spectacle. For, when the writer, in the pale grey twilight, first stepped forth upon Southern soil, the wharf was alive with the members of our party, and numerous gentlemen were returning from moonlight strolls through the city, their hands and arms laden with flowers and sprays of exquisite fragrance and verdure. A slight shower during the night had laid the dust and lent a delicious coolness to the air.

Breakfast was ordered promptly at six o'clock. This preliminary business being disposed of, we were requested by our enterprising fellow-citizen, Mr. W. E. James, to bestow ourselves as eligibly as possible upon the decks of the steamer, to be instantaneously photographed. Some of our first reflections in Charleston, were made at this moment.

It had been announced that we should have until ten o'clock for rambling about the city, at which hour, precisely, the transports would leave for Fort Sumter. The majority of the company were now waiting for the conveyances so kindly promised by Capt. Hunt, the evening previous. He had stated that the authorities had impressed all the carriages in the city for the convenience of their Northern friends. About eight o'clock, an army ambulance, drawn by a span of sorry animals, by courtesy yclept horses, was discovered approaching upon the wharf. A passenger jocularly remarked, "Here come the carriages!" whereupon a pleasant laugh went round. Soon a line of similar vehicles was drawn up alongside the Oceanus, flanked by sundry dilapidated carriages, carts, omnibusses, fish-wagons or whatever goeth upon four wheels or two, and drawn by mules, jacks and donkeys, or whatsoever goeth upon four legs or three. This was the livery of Charleston. And, surely enough, these were our carriages. With no little merriment these equipages were received, but the alacrity with which the ladies and gentlemen stowed themselves within them, showed conclusively how little they stood upon the ceremony or "order of their going."

Not from any contempt for these vehicles, but from the conviction that sight-seeing could be better accomplished in the primitive way of traveling, we set out on foot, accompanied by a few friends, and turned our footsteps into the avenue known as the Battery, when we first began to realize what war had done for the infamous city of Charleston.

The Battery is a fine and straight promenade, about a quarter of a mile in length, built directly upon the waters of the harbor. A wall of masonry rises six or seven feet to the broad esplanade or pavement of stone, commanding a magnificent prospect of the Bay, and all the fortifications therein. The street is without pavement, the stones having been used for fortifications. Upon the opposite side of the street, stand the once elegant mansions of the "aristocracy." This Battery, and these residences, four years ago were teeming with thousands of surging, frantic Charlestonians, as they witnessed the bombardment of Fort Sumter. Every foot of space in the street and upon the promenade, was occupied; every window, doorway, balcony and housetop was crowded with huzzaing Secessionists, men and women, glorying over the chivalry which pitted 10,000 armed men, under cover of strong ramparts, against seventy heroes, true to their country's flag; shut up in the narrow enclosure of a Fort and cut off by the sea from all possibility of retreat. Every shot from the doomed Sumter and from the surrounding batteries, as it went screaming to its work of demolition, or fell hissing into the sea, could be distinctly seen by the excited spectators on land; and as the fiery hail was poured without intermission for two days and a night, into that enclosure of about four acres, setting fire to the barracks and officer's quarters, and as the black smoke rose gloomily up to the heavens, or at night, was lit up by the flash of guns and the reflection of firelight, it must have seemed to one, who could read God's providences in the light of a prescient faith, as the pillar of fire and cloud which was destined to go before a race des-despised and enslaved, till it should lead them out into the promised land of liberty and peace.

And throughout those two terrible days, as long as they could serve a gun, the faithful fellows under the command of the heroic Anderson, poured forth their defiant volleys, until reason and humanity combined to dictate a surrender.

How changed now the scene! At the entrance of the Battery lies a rusty, dismounted gun upon the *débris* of an old earthwork. The crowd has fled—God only knows whither. Desolation and ruin sit monarchs of the place. Here we began to see the effect of Gen. Gilmore's shells, thrown from a distance of five and a quarter miles from the city. The splendid houses were all deserted, the glass in the windows broken, the walls dilapidated, the columns toppled over. Some had escaped with scarcely a scratch, while others were battered into shapeless ruin. Holes have been made entirely through them, from two to six feet in diameter, roofs have been broken in, sleepers uptorn and scattered, arches demolished, mantels shattered, while fragments great and small, of every description strew the floors. These were the mansions of the "*Aristocracy.*" The style of architecture is somewhat peculiar. Of many of the edifices, the main body is from three to four stories in height, with rooms very large and high. Upon *one* side, immense verandahs or piazzas with heavy columns—a verandah for each story—and all having treselated floors, must have formed the most breezy, sightly and delightful resorts for the enervate occupants. In one of these houses, a flight of eighty marble steps conducts to the upper stories. All these residences are surrounded by broad gardens, abounding yet with the most luxuriant growth of trees and shrubs—the orange, the mock orange, the magnolia, the lilac, the hawthorn, the jasmine, roses and vines of every variety. The gates were flung wide open by order of the military authorities, and we availed ourselves of the permission to pluck and carry away whatever floral trophies we desired.

Many of these gardens give evidence yet of the greatest horticultural skill and taste, though at present, of course, sadly neglected. In some parts, the growth of vegetation, trees, shrubs, vines and rose bushes was so dense and tangled that we could not force our way through by the former paths. Here and there, romantic bowers of box and hawthorn appear. Some of the rose trees grow to an astonishing height, and fairly bend with their wealth of blossoms. One rises from eight to twelve feet from the ground, bearing a rose of delicate golden tint, and of size surpassing our largest cabbage roses. And as the magnificent flowers, in their rank profusion, touch each other, and seem to melt together all over the top of the tree, they fully justify the name by which they are called "the *cloth* of *gold*." It was not yet the season for the orange and magnolia, and though we missed their spicy fragrance, we were nearly compensated by the lush and glossy greenness of their leaves. The blossoms of the mock orange were abundant.

Here we were, in the full flush of Summer, with the affluence of foliage and floral beauty all around us. We had come from the North, with only the first signs of returning Spring to be seen, in here and there a crocus and daffodil, the springing grass and the freshening green of willows in reflected heats, or along the water-courses. It was like magic. We were in another zone. The air was spiced with the aroma of flowers, and freighted with the melody of birds, all guiltless of secession, and warbling out their welcome.

But the owners of these estates—where are they? Fled—and all the proud traits of their aristocracy and superiority hushed in the streets of the silent city. They are fugitives and vagabonds, wandering up and down the interior mountains and plantations of South Carolina, indulging still the dreamy delusion, that the day is just at hand when Lee will annihilate Grant and Sherman, and then the *Confederacy* shall speak from the throne and pulpit of Charleston, its dictum of sovereignty to the States and to the world. Such was the story we were told by those who remain. But was Charleston a unanimously disloyal city throughout the four years during which the huge Rebellion was rampant? We may answer—with few exceptions—but these will be ever honored. Rev. A. P. Putnam, in his letter to the *Independent*, says:

"There is one name, at least, that will shine out

with glorious lustre in the history of these dark years of Charleston. It is that of the immortal 'PETIGRU.' From the very first, and until he died, he denounced the rebellion and its authors in most unmeasured terms of severity. Publicly and in private, he exposed the sin of treason, and proclaimed his loyalty to the Union and its flag. When asked one day by a stranger where was the Lunatic Asylum, he exclaimed, 'Every where in the city; the people are all mad!' It was a marvel that he was not assassinated. It was doubtless, only his old age, his powerful family influence, and his wide connections, that saved him. Perhaps the people regarded him as having fallen into his dotage, and were willing to tolerate one who was such an extraordinary exception to the general rule. There were others, however, in the doomed city, who were as loyal as he, but they were not in a position to utter so freely their sentiments. And of all the affecting incidents or stories connected with the war, I scarcely know of one more touching than that during the long and frightful reign of the rebellion in that birth-place of our national troubles, a small band of loyal men were wont to meet occasionally in a secret upper chamber, where with closed doors they unfurled the flag of the Stars and Stripes, and in tears, drank to its perpetual success."

The members of our company were everywhere seen emerging from these deserted houses and gardens, crossing and recrossing the streets, with boquets of fabulous dimensions in their hands, or chaffering with some little negro girl for a flower of extraordinary beauty. Passing on, we come to the South Battery, a much broader and more beautiful promenade, and resembling our city parks, with trees of lusty growth, wide walks, and parterres with flowers. At the angle, high mounds of earth had been thrown up, serving the double purpose of storehouses and magazines, and earthworks for the mounting of heavy guns. Irishmen were engaged in removing them. The only instance of animosity taking palpable form towards any of the passengers of the Oceanus, occurred at this point. One gentleman, standing a few yards from the spot, with his back to the workmen, was struck on the leg by a stone, intentionally thrown by one of these Irishmen.

Near this point still remain a seven-hundred pound Blakely gun, which the Rebels had loaded to the muzzle, and burst upon their evacuation of the city. The finest residences face the South Battery also, retaining still many evidences of their original wealth and beauty.

As we pass up Meeting and King Streets, which together with East Bay and Broad Streets, constitute the main business portion of the city, the traces of demolition become more numerous than upon the Battery. Ghastly holes appear in roofs and walls, iron doors and blinds are bent double, cornices are shivered, pavements are torn up and ploughed, making very precarious footing after nightfall. Fragments of brick and stone lie scattered on every hand. Occasionally, a face could be seen at the windows, glowering sullenly at us as we passed, but no indignity was offered, nor in any case threatened. Negroes of every shade thronged the streets; gray haired "uncles" and turbaned "aunties," grinning and giggling children, and "picaninnies," all manifesting joy to see us, in their own peculiar methods, from the quick and not disgraceful curtsey, to the frantic throwing up of the arms, clapping of hands, and the fervent exclamations of "De Lord bress ye, we so powerful glad you've come!" Some of their welcomes were really affecting, and many a visitor that day listened with emotion to their simple stories of suffering, and their rude but cordial expression of greeting.

Advancing along these streets, we come to the district burned in 1861. That fire consumed nearly a fifth part of the city. These ruins, which no attempt has been made to rebuild, stand in all their desolateness, increased by the havoc of the bombardment The tall chimneys, grim and charred, the dilapidated walls, overgrown with moss, the cellars, rank with grass, weeds and thistles, the streets without pavement, and ankle-deep with sand, are a startling commentary upon the accounts with which we were favored during the war, by the Charleston papers, to the following effect:

"The Yankees continue to shell the city, with about the usual consequences, of here and there a chimney toppled over, and a negro badly frightened, but with no actual damage." Now we saw that the entire lower and business part of the city must have been as deserted as the ruins of Herculaneum.

All the grandees, who flaunted in their pride of wealth and caste, and flogged their negroes irresponsibly, coining every dollar out of the "unrequited" sweat and blood of their bondmen, have fled penniless and ruined into the interior, while in a strange, yet ever righteous revolution of the wheels of retributive justice, these same negroes, now "free as I am," nestle in the ancient homes, and hold their fantastic jubilees in the self-same halls, which once echoed to their oppressor's revels. A very few have returned, and possess their old homesteads, having taken the oath of allegiance, some heartily and to receive the kindly protection of our forces, but the majority only through fear, and to save what little property the Rebel government had left them. Many a Southern "gentleman," who four years ago, rejoiced in his thousands, is to day a vagabond; or, if still remaining in the city, professedly loyal, is a pauper and beneficiary, on a level with the most wretched contraband who sues for alms as you pass.

Concerning the condition of the inhabitants, Rev. Mr. Cuyler, thus writes to the "*Evangelist*."

"With the exception of a few blockade-running speculators, who sent their profits abroad for investment, the merchants and planters of Charleston are hopelessly bankrupt. We saw the cashier of the bank of Charleston come up to the commissary's door, and receive his pittance of bread and rice for his daily food, just as the refugee negroes were doing a few doors off. We went through Secretary Memminger's deserted and once splendid mansion; the remaining contraband told us 'Massa Memmenger sent his money over to Europe; he be up in Nort Carolina; he be rich to-day.' A gentleman in Charleston, says that he saw in the books of a bank in Havana, the sum of $100,000 in gold, credited to Jefferson Davis. Gov. Aiken, told me that if this were so, it must be the gift of friends, for said he, "Mr. Davis spent all his salary, and is considered poor." Not only is Charleston aristocracy bankrupt, but most of them are dead. Gov. Aiken said, sadly enough: 'our most wealthy young men enlisted, many of them as privates, they are nearly all dead or in prison; South Carolina has among her whites, nobody left but old men and little boys.' Truly the iron has entered into Charleston's proud soul, and she is the most blasted, blighted, broken-hearted desolation on this continent. Her cup of misery is filled to the brim. I could not exult over her woeful wretchedness, although I felt that it was not one whit more than her stupendous sin has richly deserved. She has lived on the spoils of the plundered bondmen; now her turn has come for the bondmen to dwell in the deserted places of the slave-ocrat. Robert Small, the famous negro captain of the steamboat "Planter," (who has now a salary of $1,800 as her commander,) is able to give bread to half the bank-presidents and brokers of Broad St."

Upon some of the houses, we found placards to the following effect:

"Safe-guard—Protection is hereby given to the property of———he—or *she*—generally the latter—having taken the oath of allegiance."

"This house is occupied by the permission of the Provost-Marshal."

"Taken—by consent of the authorities."

"To be occupied by the owner, who has taken the oath of allegiance to the United States."

In the windows, or upon the doors of the business-houses or shops, licenses were posted, declaring that the occupant, who had taken the oath, or paid the fee required by act of Congress, might carry on the business.

Our examination of the city, during the two hours allotted, was necessarily cursory. The time had elapsed, and now the passengers were to be seen returning from every direction, laden with flowers of richest hue and odor, and lugging together various mementoes and relics gathered among the gardens and public buildings. As the chronological order of arrangement in this work is the most simple and natural, it will be followed, though apparently at the sacrifice of unity. We shall therefore return, in a succeeding chapter, to a more minute description of scenes and incidents in the city of Charleston.

CHAPTER V.

LEAVING the Oceanus at the wharf at ten o'clock, we embarked on the transport "Golden Gate," for Fort Sumter. The scene in the harbor was gay beyond description. The "Canonicus," a Government vessel, crowded in every part by the "boys" in blue pants and jackets, first headed up the bay towards the fort. Lines of flags, and signals of every color and combination of colors, scores and hundreds in number, stretched from bowsprit to foremast, from foremast to main, from main to mizzen, and from mizzen to stern; crossed and festooned from yard to yard, and upon all the rigging, made the vessel a blaze of prismatic brilliancy. The "Blackstone," a very large screw-steamer, decked with equal profusion of bunting and beauty, next rounded majestically into broader waters. Then followed the "Delaware" and "Robert Coit," Government transports, bearing their burden of rejoicing and eager patriots. Almost central in interest, the "Planter," crowded almost to suffocation upon her three decks, with Gen. Saxton's freedmen, revealed her splashing paddles through the broken wheelhouse. Another such a motley crew will seldom if ever be seen. Grey-haired old men, whose wrinkles were lighted up with deep but quiet joy; middle-aged men and women, of every grade of color possible to Southern civilization, the latter decorated with bandanas and turbans of flashy colors; comely and buxom girls attired in neat chintz; cadaverous and ragged beings holding about them their tattered garments; boys and girls whose jubilation exhibited itself in the most astonishing display of ivory;—all huddled together like sheep in a pen, hanging over the gunwales, mounted on the posts, doubled up in furtive corners, peering through the gangways, darkening the wheel-house, upon the top of which stood Robert Small, a prince among them, self-possessed, prompt and proud, giving his orders to the helmsman in ringing tones of command.

An unaccountable delay occurred in the starting of the "Golden Gate." But we allayed our impatience by studying and enjoying the splendid spectacular drama now being enacted in the harbor. Guns were booming, bells ringing, bands playing the most enlivening patriotic airs, men and women were cheering and singing, while we awaited our sailing orders from the captain. A stiff breeze was blowing from the westward, throwing up the white caps, and fluttering into cheerful music the folds of the innumerable flags. The wharves on every side were crowded with eager witnesses. At length the wheels moved, and we passed through the midst of the anchored fleet, upon one of which we counted over three hundred signals and banners, over all

FORT SUMTER—INTERIOR VIEW.

of which, wherever displayed, waved the unapproachably beautiful and ever superior flag of "Stripes and Stars."

For half an hour or more, we lay rocking upon the swell, while one and another transport landed its load at the dock of the fort. We passed the time in studying the storied old ruin. A *ruin* it is, though not so utter, as the imaginations of some artists have depicted it. It is built externally of brick, and filled in with stone, sand and earth. The walls are deeply indented by the shot hurled against it; the top lines are uneven, and in some parts battered half way down towards the foundation. As it was terribly bombarded, while in Rebel possession, and its walls gave way by day, by night the Rebels piled cylindrical baskets filled with sand in all the chasms, and now they rise in rows or layers six or seven deep, nearly to the original height. The casemates are filled with the broken stone and brick, and the most of the port-holes closed. Around it, upon the rocks, is a stratum of balls, exploded shells and comminuted brick, to the depth of several inches.

The signal being given for the "Golden Gate" to approach, in five minutes we are at the landing; the same at which Wigfall, the self-appointed commissioner to propose terms to Major Anderson, landed in 1861, from a row-boat. On either side of the platform, upon which we debark, was a company of soldiers, with muskets shouldered and bayonets fixed—on the left, white, on the right, black, rivalling each other in soldierly bearing. We ascended to the top of the wall, by a flight of fifty steps, passed under an arbor entrance of evergreens, walked across about thirty feet of earth and sand, and lo! the interior of the glorious old fort appears in view — glorious yet, though in ruins. Immediately in the centre was the new flag-staff, surmounted by circular terraces of grass, and these surmounted by immense conical shot and shell, planted with the points upward. Before the flag-staff, was a large platform carpeted with myrtle, mock-orange, and evergreen boughs, the railings festooned and twined with the same. Four pillars, fifteen feet in height, rose from the corners of the platform, wound with the national colors, and knotted with orange wreaths, while from their tops, graceful arches were sprung, terminating together in the centre. Upon the very apex was a golden eagle, standing upon the flying flag. Rows of substantial seats surrounded the platform, which we found already nearly filled. The interior of the fort presented the appearance of a huge earthwork, for as the sides were slowly demolished, the shattered stones and sand fell down in slanting grade towards the centre, and now remain as they were found. Surmounting the parapet towards Charleston were six large guns, ready for the grand salute. The crowd now gathered densely, but were admirably disposed and managed by Col. Stuart L. Woodford, who was in charge of the exercises of the day.

While waiting for the arrival of the orator of the day with his party, the flag of the "Planter" was seen above the parapet, slowly waving towards the landing, and was greeted with cheers.

Mr. Wm. B. Bradbury, taking a position at the foot of the flag-staff, then led the whole multitude in singing his resounding song, "*Victory at Last*," which was followed by "*Rally Round the Flag*."

A few minutes later, the passengers from the "Arago" were brought to the landing, by the "Delaware," and were seen crossing the sandy parapet and descending the stairway, into the fort. As one and another familiar face was discovered, signs of recognition were given, breaking out, in two or three instances, into ringing cheers.

Upon the platform, salutations were exchanged for a few moments; and, all preliminaries having been duly arranged, the exercises of the day were begun and carried forward according to the pre-arranged programme, as will now be set forth.

Breathless was the attention with which the venerable man was received, who was to offer the

1. Introductory Prayer.

Rev. Matthias Harris, Chaplain U. S. Army, who made the prayer at the raising of the Flag, when Major Anderson removed his command to Fort Sumter, Dec. 27, 1860, now stepped slowly to the front of the platform, uncovered his head, silvered with age, and while his thin locks streamed in the wind, read a brief, but appropriate prayer, with trembling voice, which he closed with much emotion, pronouncing a blessing upon the flag of his fathers.

Rev. R. S. Storrs, Jr., D. D., of Brooklyn, N. Y., then advanced, and with sonorous and solemn voice, read the following:

2. Selection from the Psalms.

(The assembly making the responses.)

PSALM 126.

1. When the Lord turned again the captivity of Zion, we were like them that dream.

2. Then was our mouth filled with laughter and our tongue with singing: then said they among the heathen, The Lord hath done great things for them.

3. The Lord hath done great things for us, whereof we are glad.

4. Turn again our captivity, O Lord, as the streams in the south.

5. They that sow in tears, shall reap in joy.

6. He that goeth forth and weepeth, bearing precious seed, shall doubtless come again with rejoicing, bringing his sheaves with him.

PSALM 47.

1. O clap your hands; all ye people, shout unto God with the voice of triumph.

2. For the Lord most high is terrible; he is a great King above all the earth.

3. He shall subdue the people under us, and the nations under our feet.

4. He shall choose our inheritance for us, the excellency of Jacob whom he loved.

5. God is gone up with a shout, the Lord with the sound of a trumpet.

6. Sing praises to God, sing praises; sing praises unto our King, sing praises.

7. For God is the King of all the earth; sing ye praises with understanding.

8. God reigneth over the heathen; God sitteth upon the throne of his holiness.

9. The princes of the people are gathered together, even the people of the God of Abraham; for the shields of the earth belong unto God; He is greatly exalted.

PSALM 98.

1. O sing unto the Lord a new song: for he hath done marvelous things: his right hand and his holy arm hath gotten him the victory.

2. The Lord hath made known his salvation: his righteousness hath he openly shewed in the sight of the heathen.

3. He hath remembered his mercy and truth toward the House of Israel: all the ends of the earth have seen the salvation of our God.

4. Make a joyful noise unto the Lord, all the earth: make a loud noise and rejoice and sing praises.

5. Sing unto the Lord with the harp: with the harp and the voice of a psalm.

6. With trumpets and sound of cornet, make a joyful noise before the Lord, the King.

7. Let the sea roar and the fulness thereof: the world and they that dwell therein.

8. Let the floods clap their hands: let the hills be joyful together

9. Before the Lord: for he cometh to judge the earth: with righteousness shall he judge the world and the people with equity.

PART OF PSALM 20.

(Read by Minister and people together.)

Some trust in chariots, and some in horses, but we will remember the Name of the Lord our God.

We will rejoice in Thy salvation, and in the *Name of our God*, WE WILL SET UP OUR BANNERS!

Minister—Glory be to the Father, and to the Son, and to the Holy Ghost:

Answer—As it was in the beginning, is now, and ever shall be, world without end. Amen.

3. Major Anderson's Despatch

to the Government, dated Steamship Baltic, off Sandy Hook, April 18, 1861, announcing the fall of Fort Sumter, was read by Brevet Brigadier-General E. D. Townsend, Assistant Adjutant-General, U. S. A.

4. "RAISING AND PLANTING UPON THE RUINS OF FORT SUMTER THE SAME UNITED STATES FLAG which floated over the battlements of the Fort during the rebel assault, April 14, 1861, by Brevet Major-General Robert Anderson, U. S. A. As soon as the flag is raised, a salute of one hundred guns will be fired from Fort Sumter, and a national salute from every fort and rebel battery that fired upon Fort Sumter. The band will play national airs."

Thus it was announced upon the programme for the day.

But Heaven forbid that we should pass this wonderful, soul-thrilling event, without more extended notice!

As soon as Gen. Townsend had finished reading Major Anderson's Despatch, Sergeant Hart brought forward a new mail-bag, which contained the original flag. The first glimpse of the precious emblem, as it came forth to the light once more from its long and carefully guarded seclusion, was the signal for the most tumultuous cheers. It was made fast to the halyards by three of the crew of the "Juniata," with a beautiful wreath of evergreens, thickly studded with roses and blossoms of the mock-orange, just above it.

General Anderson stood by it upon the terrace. Commingled joy and sadness struggled upon his manly face. His hair, thickly sprinkled with grey, was stirred by the winds upon his uncovered head. His erect, soldierly form was the centre of every gaze. For a moment, he spoke not. He seemed wrestling with intense emotion, as if living over again, in that moment, the terrible scenes of four years before, and as if conscious that through the ten thousand eyes of that vast assemblage, the whole nation was looking at him. At length, with subdued voice and scarcely mastered emotion, he spoke as follows:

"I am here my friends, my fellow-citizens, and fellow soldiers, to perform an act of duty to my country dear to my heart, and which all of you will appreciate and feel. Had I observed the wishes of my heart, it should have been done in silence: but in accordance with the request of the Honorable Secretary of War, I make a few remarks, as by his order, after four long, long years of war, I restore to its proper place this flag which floated here during peace, before the first act of this cruel Rebellion. (Here taking the halyards in his hands, he proceeded.) I thank God that I have lived to see this day, and to be here to perform this, perhaps the last act of my life, of duty to my country.

"I thank God who has so signally blessed us, who has blessed us beyond measure. May all the nations bless and praise the name of the Lord, and proclaim 'Glory to God in the highest, and on earth peace, good will towards men.'"

As the voice of the General, the hero of the hour was borne away upon the air, he grasped the halyards, and with strong and steady pull, lifted the nation's symbol from the green turf, and as the old smoke-stained, shot-pierced flag, with not a single star smitten or effaced from its fold of blue, rose slowly upward to its native air, and its folds were caught by the ocean breeze as in joyous welcome again, the whole multitude, citizens, soldiers, officers, that filled the interior, and sat upon the sandy slopes and parapet of the fort, by a spontaneous and irrepressible impulse, rose to their feet, waived hats and handkerchiefs with frantic exultation above their heads, and with one long, pealing, deafening, ecxtatic shout of triumph hailed the dear flag until it touched the peak. Senators, Generals, Clergymen, Editors and Civilians upon the platform, to whom the end of the halyards was passed, surged away upon it as though their hands alone were lifting "Old Glory" to it place. The excited multitude wrung each other's hands in joy, huzzahed until they were hoarse, wept and laughed by turns, and when the song broke forth,

"The star-spangled banner, O long may it wave!
O'er the land of the free, and the home of the brave!"

tears of gladness filled every eye, and flowed down cheeks unused to weeping, and in the seething jubilant throng and melting weltering chorus of five thousand voices, we seemed to discover no inapt type and foreshadowing of the vast multitude which shall stand upon the sea of glass, having the harps of God, and singing "Great and marvellous are thy works,

THE RAISING OF THE FLAG.

Lord God Almighty; just and true are thy ways, thou King of Saints!"

And the flag itself, as if true to its instincts and mission, flung its emblematic folds directly over the waters of the harbor, and towards the conquered city of Charleston. That cradle of the Rebellion cannot escape the domination of the "flag of the free heart's hope and home!"

The instant the banner touched the peak, the six guns upon the parapet of Sumter, looking towards Charleston, pealed forth their detonations.

Then, answering, from all the surrounding fortifications—Forts Moultrie, Ripley, Pinckney, Putnam, Johnson, Cumming's Point, Battery Bee — from every battery that took part in the bombardment of Fort Sumter in 1861, and from all the vessels of war in the harbor, came the thunder of mighty cannon, in national salute, until the "earth shook and trembled," and the air grew dark with the gathering clouds of smoke which rolled their dun and murky volume over the harbor, shutting out from sight at length the city, and the lightning flash of the cannonade.

There was a general stampede from the interior, to the walls of the fort, that the sense of sight as well as of hearing, might be gratified. Those who were first upon this outlook describe the cordon of fire by which they were surrounded as something startlingly magnificent. But those who reached the parapet later returned disappointed, for it was only like looking into a bank of fog, and the sand, stirred up by the recoil of Fort Sumter's guns, was driven into their eyes in blinding clouds. They were glad to resume their seats, and at the expiration of the salute, which lasted about half an hour, compose themselves to listen to the next grand exercise upon the programme.

6. The Address, by the Rev. Henry Ward Beecher.

As Mr. Beecher came forward upon the platform, he was greeted with a round of cheers. This Rev. gentleman, who has contended with foemen of almost every kind, found two antagonists awaiting him, which, with his usual dexterity, he baffled upon this occasion. These were his manuscript, in detached leaves, and a strong northwesterly wind. At first onset, he removed his grey felt hat from his head, and held his MSS. in his left hand. But the indiscriminate wind toyed so familiarly with his iron-grey ear-locks, and played such fantasias upon the thin leaves of his address, that he placed his errant locks again in confinement, and addressed himself with both hands to his refractory documents. He had conquered.

Mr. Beecher *read* his entire oration, pausing once midway, to rest his overtaxed voice, while the band played a patriotic air.

The address was carefully composed, and thoroughly considered. Clearness and force marked all its periods. The principles laid down were emphatic, and almost exhaustive. The policy of the Government was sharply defined, and the feeling of the people faithfully represented.

In delivery, it lacked the peculiar magnetism of his less studied efforts, but his decision to commit all his thoughts to paper, commended itself to every better judgment. From beginning to end, he seemed deeply impressed with the consciousness that he was speaking, at least, semi-officially, and that his utterances would be regarded, not only as the voice of the authorities at the Capital, and of all the nation, but would pass from that hour into history. But as a verbatim report of the entire address is here introduced, every reader of this volume may become his own commentator.

It has already been widely circulated, and universally read, and is included within these pages, not to give to *it* publicity, but that *they* may have, at least, one adornment, and because their humble record would be sadly incomplete without it.

THE ADDRESS.

On this solemn and joyful day, we again lift to the breeze, our father's flag, now, again, the banner of *the United States*, with the fervent prayer that God would crown it with honor, protect it from treason, and send it down to our children, with all the blessings of civilization, liberty and religion. Terrible in battle, may it be beneficent in peace. Happily, no bird or beast of prey has been inscribed upon it. The stars that redeem the night from darkness, and the beams of red light that beautify the morning, have been united upon its folds. As long as the sun endures, or the stars, may it wave over a nation neither enslaved nor enslaving. (Great applause.) Once, and but once, has treason dishonored it. In that insane hour, when the guiltiest and bloodiest rebellion of time hurled their fires upon this fort, you, sir, (turning to General Anderson) and a small heroic band, stood within these now crumbled walls, and did gallant and just battle for the honor and defence of the nation's banner. (Applause.)

In that cope of fire this glorious flag still peacefully waved to the breeze above your head, unconscious of harm as the stars and skies above it. Once it was shot down. A gallant hand, in whose care this day it has been, plucked it from the ground, and reared it again,—"cast down but not destroyed." After a vain resistance, with trembling hand and sad heart, you withdrew it from its height, closed its wings, and bore it far away, sternly to sleep amid the tumults of rebellion and the thunder of battle. The first act of war had begun. The long night of four years had set in. While the giddy traitors whirled in a maze of exhileration, dim horrors were already advancing, that were ere long to fill the land with blood.

To-day you are returned again. We devoutly join with you in thanksgiving to Almighty God, that he has spared your honored life, and vouchsafed you the honors of this day. The heavens over you are the same; the same shores; morning comes, and evening, as they did. All else, how changed! What grim batteries crowd the burdened shores! What scenes have filled this air and disturbed these waters! These shattered heaps of shapeless stone are all that is left of Fort Sumter. Desolation broods in yonder sad city—solemn retribution hath avenged our dishonored banner! You have come back with honor, who departed hence, four years ago, leaving the air sultry with fanaticism. The surging crowds that rolled up their frenzied shouts, as the flag came down, are dead, or scattered, or silent; and their habitations are desolate. Ruin sits in the cradle of treason. Rebellion has perished. But, there flies the same flag that was insulted. (Great and prolonged applause.) With starry eyes it looks all over this bay for that banner that supplanted it, and sees it not. (Applause.) You that then, for the day, were humbled, are here again, to triumph once and forever. (Applause.) In the storm of that assault this glorious ensign was often struck; but, memorable fact, not one of its *stars* was torn out, by shot or shell. (Applause.) It was a prophecy.

It said: "Not one State shall be struck from this nation by treason!" (Applause.) The fulfillment is at hand. Lifted to the air, to-day, it proclaims, after four years of war, "Not a State is blotted out!" (Applause.)

Hail to the flag of our fathers, and our flag! Glory to the banner that has gone through four years black with tempests of war, to pilot the nation back to peace without dismemberment! And glory be to God, who, above all hosts and banners, hath ordained victory, and shall ordain peace! (Applause.)

Wherefore have we come hither, pilgrims from distant places? Are we come to exult that Northern hands are stronger than Southern? No, but to rejoice that the hands of those who defend a just and beneficent government are mightier than the hands that assaulted it! (Applause.) Do we exult over fallen cities? We exult that a Nation has not fallen. (Applause.) We sorrow with the sorrowful. We sympathize with the desolate. We look upon this shattered fort, and yonder dilapidated city, with sad eyes, grieved that men should have committed such treason, and glad that God hath set such a mark upon treason that all ages shall dread and abhor it. (Applause.)

We exult, not for a passion gratified, but for a sentiment victorious; not for temper, but for conscience; not as we devoutly believe that *our* will is done, but that God's will hath been done. We should be unworthy of that liberty entrusted to our care, if, on a such a day as this, we sullied our hearts by feelings of aimless vengeance; and equally unworthy, if we did not devoutly thank Him who hath said, *Vengeance is mine, I will repay, saith the Lord*, that he hath set a mark upon arrogant Rebellion, ineffaceable while time lasts!

Since this flag went down on that dark day, who shall tell the mighty woes that have made this land a spectacle to angels and men? The soil has drunk blood, and is glutted. Millions mourn for millions slain; or, envying the dead, pray for oblivion. Towns and villages have been razed. Fruitful fields have turned back to wilderness. It came to pass, as the prophet said: *The sun was turned to darkness, and the moon to blood.* The course of law was ended. The sword sat chief magistrate in half the nation; industry was paralyzed; morals corrupted; the public weal invaded by rapine and anarchy; whole States ravaged by avenging armies. The world was amazed. The earth reeled. When the flag sank here, it was as if political night had come, and all beasts of prey had come forth to devour.

That long night is ended! And for this returning day we have come from afar, to rejoice and give thanks. No more war! No more accursed secession! No more slavery, that spawned them both! (Great applause.)

Let no man misread the meaning of this unfolding flag! It says, "GOVERNMENT hath returned hither." It proclaims in the name of vindicated government, peace and protection to loyalty; humiliation and pains to traitors. This is the flag of sovereignty. The nation, not the States, is sovereign. Restored to authority, this flag commands, not supplicates.

There may be pardon, but no concession. (Great applause.) There may be amnesty and oblivion, but no honied compromises. (Applause.) The nation to-day has peace for the peaceful, and war for the turbulent. (Applause.) The only condition of submission, is, *to submit!* (Laughter and applause.) There is the Constitution, there are the laws, there is the Government. They rise up like mountains of strength that shall not be moved. *They are the conditions of peace.*

One nation, under one government, without slavery, has been ordained, and shall stand. There can be peace on no other basis. On this basis reconstruction is easy, and needs neither architect or engineer. Without this basis no engineer or architect shall ever reconstruct these rebellious States.

We do not want your cities nor your fields. We do not envy you your prolific soil, nor heavens full of perpetual summer. Let agriculture revel here; let manufactures make every stream twice musical; build fleets in every port; inspire the arts of peace with genius second only to that of Athens; and we shall be glad in your gladness, and rich in your wealth.

All that we ask is unswerving loyalty, and universal liberty. (Applause.) And that, in the name of this *high sovereignty of the United States of America*, we demand; and that, with the blessing of Almighty God, *we will have!* (Great applause.)

We raise our Father's banner that it may bring back better blessings than those of old; that it may cast out the devil of discord; that it may restore lawful government, and a prosperity purer and more enduring than that which it protected before; that it may win parted friends from their alienation; that it may inspire hope, and inaugurate universal liberty; that it may say to the sword, "*Return to thy sheath*," and to the plow and sickle, "*Go forth*;" that it may heal all jealousies, unite all policies, inspire a new national life, compact our strength, purify our principles, ennoble our national ambitions, and make this people great and strong, not for aggression and quarrelsomeness, but for *the peace of the world*, giving to us the glorious prerogative of leading all nations to juster laws, to more humane policies, to sincerer friendship, to rational, instituted civil liberty, and to universal Christian brotherhood.

Reverently, piously, in hopeful patriotism, we spread this banner on the sky, as of old the bow was planted on the cloud; and, with solemn fervor, beseech God to look upon it, and make it the memorial of an everlasting covenant and decree, that never again on this fair land shall a deluge of blood prevail. (Applause.)

Why need any eye turn from this spectacle? Are there not associations which, overleaping the recent past, carry us back to times when, over North and South, this flag was honored alike by all? In all our colonial days, we were one; in the long Revolutionary struggle; and in the scores of prosperous years succeeding. When the passage of the Stamp Act in 1765 aroused the colonies, it was Gadsden of South Carolina that cried with prescient enthusiasm: "*We stand on the broad common ground of those natural rights that we all feel and know as men.* There ought to be no New England man, no New Yorker, known on this continent, but all of us," said he, "AMERICANS." That *was* the voice of South Carolina. That *shall be* the voice of South Carolina. Faint is the echo; but it is coming. We now hear it sighing sadly through the pines; but it shall yet break upon the shore—no North, no West, no South, but one United States of America. (Applause.)

There is scarcely a man born in the South who has lifted his hand against this banner, but had a father who would have died for it. Is memory dead? Is there no historic pride? Has a fatal fury struck blindness or hate into eyes that used to look kindly toward each other; that read the same Bible; that hung over the same historic pages of our national glory; that studied the same Constitution?

Let this uplifting bring back all of the past that was good, but leave in darkness all that was bad.

It was never before so wholly unspotted; so clear of all wrong; so purely and simply the sign of Justice and Liberty. Did I say that we brought back the same banner that you bore away, noble and heroic sir? It is not the same. It is more and better than it was. The land is free from slavery, since that banner fell.

When God would prepare Moses for Emancipation, he overthrew his first steps, and drove him for forty years to brood in the wilderness. When our flag came down, four years it lay brooding in darkness. It cried to the Lord, "Wherefore am I deposed?" Then arose before it a vision of its sin. It had strengthened the strong, and forgotten the weak. It proclaimed liberty, but trod upon slaves.

In that seclusion it dedicated itself to liberty. Behold, to-day, it fulfills its vows? When it went down four million people had no flag. To-day it rises, and four million people cry out, "Behold *our* flag?" Hark! they murmur. It is the Gospel that they recite in sacred words; "It is a Gospel to the poor, it heals our broken hearts, it preaches deliverance to captives, it gives sight to the blind, it sets at liberty them that are bruised." Rise up, then, glorious Gospel Banner, and roll out these messages of God. Tell the air that not a spot now sullies thy whiteness. Thy red is not the blush of shame, but the flush of joy. Tell the dews that wash thee that thou art pure as they. Say to the night, that thy stars lead toward the morning; and to the morning, that a brighter day arises with healing in its wings. And then, oh glorious flag, bid the sun pour light on all thy folds with double brightness, whilst thou art bearing around and round the world the solemn joy—a race set free! a nation redeemed!

The mighty hand of Government, made strong in war, by the favor of the God of Battles, spreads wide to-day the banner of liberty that went down in darkness, that arose in light; and there it streams, like the sun above it, neither parceled out nor monopolized, but flooding the air with light for all mankind. Ye scattered and broken, ye wounded and dying, bitten by the fiery serpents of oppression, everywhere, in all the world, look upon this sign, lifted up, and live. And ye homeless and houseless slaves, look, and ye are free. At length *you*, too, have part and lot in this glorious ensign, that broods with impartial love over small and great, the poor and the strong, the bond and the free.

In this solemn hour, let us pray for the quick coming of reconciliation and happiness, under this common flag!

But, we must build again, from the foundations, in all these now free Southern States. No cheap exhortation "to forgetfulness of the past, to restore all things as they were," will do. God does not stretch out his hand, as he has for four dreadful years, that men may easily forget the might of his terrible acts. Restore things as they were? What, the alienations and jealousies? The discords and contentions, and the causes of them? No. In that solemn sacrifice on which a nation has offered up for its sins so many precious victims, loved and lamented, let our sins and mistakes be consumed utterly and forever.

No, never again shall things be restored as before the war. It is written in God's decree of events fulfilled, "Old things are passed away." That new earth, in which dwelleth righteousness, draws near.

Things as they were? Who has an omnipotent hand to restore a million dead, slain in battle, or wasted by sickness, or dying of grief, broken-hearted? Who has omniscience, to search for the scattered ones? Who shall restore the lost to broken families? Who shall bring back the squandered treasure, the years of industry wasted, and convince you that four years of guilty rebellion, and cruel war, are no more than dirt upon the hand, which a moment's washing removes, and leaves the hand clean as before? Such a war reaches down to the very vitals of society.

Emerging from such a prolonged rebellion, he is blind who tells you that the State, by a mere amnesty and benevolence of Government, can be put again, by a mere decree, in its old place. It would not be honest, it would not be kind or fraternal, for me to pretend that Southern revolution against the Union, has not reacted, and wrought revolution in the Southern States themselves, and inaugurated a new dispensation.

Society is like a broken loom, and the piece which rebellion put in, and was weaving, has been cut, and every thread broken. You must put in new warp and new woof—and, weaving anew, as the fabric slowly unwinds, we shall see in it no gorgon figures, no hideous grotesques of the old barbarism, but the figures of liberty, vines and golden grains, framing in the heads of Justice, Love, and Liberty!

The august Convention of 1787, framed the Constitution with this memorable preamble: "We, the people of the United States, in order to form a more perfect Union, establish justice, insure domestic tranquility, provide for the common defence, promote the general welfare, and secure the blessings of liberty to ourselves and our posterity, do ordain this Constitution for the United States of America."

Again, in the awful Convention of war, the people of the United States, for the very ends just recited, have debated, settled and ordained, certain fundamental truths, which must henceforth be accepted and obeyed. Nor is any State, or any individual wise, who shall disregard them. They are to civil affairs, what the natural laws are to health—indispensable conditions of peace and happiness.

What are the ordinances given by the people, speaking out of fire and darkness of war, with authority inspired by that same God, who gave the laws from Sinai amid thunders and trumpet voices?

1. That these United States shall be one and indivisible.

2. That States are not absolute sovereigns, and have no right to dismember the republic.

3. That universal liberty is indispensable to Republican Government, and that slavery shall be utterly and forever abolished?

Such are the results of war! These are the best fruits of the war. They are worth all they have cost. They are foundations of peace. They will secure benefits to all nations, as well as to us.

Our highest wisdom and duty is to accept the facts, as the decrees of God. We are exhorted to forget all that has happened. Yes, the wrath, the conflict, the cruelty, but not those overruling decrees of God, which this war has pronounced. As solemnly as on Mount Sinai, God says, "Remember! *remember!*" Hear it, to-day. Under this sun, under that bright child of the sun, our banner, with the eyes of this nation and of the world upon us, we repeat the syllables of God's Providence, and recite the solemn decrees:

No more Disunion!

No more Secession!

No more Slavery! (Applause.)

Why did this civil war begin?

We do not wonder that European statesmen failed to comprehend this conflict, and foreign philanthropists were shocked at a murderous war, that seemed to have had no moral origin; but, like the brutal fights of beasts of prey, to have sprung from ferocious animalism. This great nation, filling all profitable latitudes, cradled between two oceans, with inexhaustible resources, with riches increasing in an unparalleled ratio, by agriculture, by manufactures, by commerce, with schools and churches, with books and newspapers, thick as leaves in our own forests, with institutions sprung from the people, and peculiarly adapted to their genius; a nation not sluggish, but active, used to excitement, practiced in political wisdom, and accustomed to self-government, and all its vast outlying parts held together by a federal government, mild in temper, gentle in administration, and beneficent in results, we do not wonder that it is not understood abroad.

All at once, in this hemisphere of happiness and hope, there came trooping clouds with fiery bolts, full of death and desolation. At a cannon shot upon this fort, all the nation, as if they had been a trained army lying on their arms, awaiting a signal, rose up and began a war which for awfulness, rises into the first rank of bad eminence. The front of battle, going with the sun, was twelve hundred miles long; and the depth, measured along a meridian, was a thousand miles. In this vast area, more than two million men, first and last, for four years, have in skirmish, fight and battle, met in more than a thousand conflicts; while a coast and river line, not less than four thousand miles in length, has swarmed with fleets, freighted with artillery. The very industry of the country seemed to have been touched by some infernal wand, and with one wheel, changed its front from peace to war. The anvils of the land beat like drums. As out of the ooze emerge monsters, so from our mines and founderies uprose new and strange machines of war, iron-clad.

And so, in a nation of peaceful habits, without external provocation, there arose such a storm of war, as blackened the whole horizon and hemisphere. What wonder that foreign observers stood amazed at this fanatical fury, that seemed without divine guidance, but inspired wholly with infernal frenzy?

The explosion was sudden, but the train had long been laid. We must consider the condition of Southern society, if we would understand the mystery of this iniquity. Society in the South, resolves itself into three divisions, more sharply distinguished than in any other part of the nation. At the base is the laboring class, made up of slaves. Next is the middle class, made up of traders, small farmers, and poor men. The lower edge of this class touched the slave, and the upper edge reached up to the third and ruling class. This class were a small minority in numbers, but in practiced ability, they had centered in their hands the whole government of the South, and had mainly governed the country.

Upon this polished, cultured, exceedingly capable and wholly unprincipled class, rests the whole burden of this war. Forced up by the bottom heat of slavery, the ruling class, in all the disloyal States, arrogated to themselves a superiority not compatible with republican equality, nor with just morals. They claimed a right of pre-eminence. An evil prophet arose who trained these wild and luxuriant shoots of ambition to the shapely form of a political philosophy.

By its re-agents they precipitated drudgery to the bottom of society, and left at the top what they thought to be a clarified fluid. In their political economy, labor was to be owned by capital. In their theory of government, a few were to rule the many. They boldly avowed, not the fact alone, that under all forms of government, the few rule the many, but their right and duty to do so. Set free from the necessity of labor, they conceived a contempt for those who felt its wholesome regimen. Believing themselves foreordained to supremacy, they regarded the popular vote, when it failed to register their wishes, as an intrusion and a nuisance. They were born in a garden, and popular liberty, like freshets, overswelling their banks, but covered their dainty walks and flowers with slime and mud—of Democratic votes. (Applause).

When, with shrewd observation, they saw the growth of the popular element in the Northern States, they instinctively took in the inevitable events. It must be controlled, or cut off from a nation governed by gentlemen! Controlled, less and less, could it be, in every decade; and they prepared secretly, earnestly, and with wide conference and mutual connivance.

We are to distinguish between the pretences, and means, and causes of this war.

To inflame and unite the great middle class of the South, who had no interest in separation, and no business with war, they alleged grievances that never existed, and employed arguments which they better than all other men, knew to be specious and false. Slavery itself was cared for only as an instrument of power, or of excitement. They had unalterably fixed their eyes upon empire, and all was good which would secure that, and bad which hindered it.

Thus, the ruling class of the South—an aristocracy as intense, proud and inflexible as ever existed—not limited either by customs or institutions, not recognized and adjusted in the regular order of society, playing a reciprocal part in its machinery, but secretly disowning its own existence, baptized with ostentatious names of democracy, obsequious to the people for the sake of governing them; this nameless, lurking aristocracy, that ran in the blood of society like a rash, not yet come to the skin; this political tapeworm, that produced nothing, but lay coiled in the body, feeding on its nutriment, and holding the whole structure but a servant set up to nourish it—this aristocracy of the plantation, with firm and deliberate resolve, brought on the war, that they might cut the land in two; and clearing themselves from incorrigible free society, set up a sterner, statelier empire, where slaves worked that gentlemen might live at ease. Nor can there be any doubt that though, at first, they meant to erect the form of republican government, this was but a device; a step necessary to the securing of that power by which they should be able to change the whole economy of society.

That they never dreamed of such a war, we may well believe. That they would have accepted it, though twice as bloody, if only thus they could rule, none can doubt that knows the temper of these worst men of modern society. (Applause). But, they miscalculated. They understood the people of the South; but they were totally incapable of understanding the character of the great working classes of the loyal States. That industry which is the foundation of independence, and so of equity, they stigmatized as stupid drudgery, or as mean avarice. That general intelligence and independence of thought, which schools for the common people and newspapers breed, they reviled as the incitement of unsettled zeal, running easily into fanaticism.

They more thoroughly misunderstood the profound sentiment of loyalty; the deep love of country which pervaded the common people. If those who knew them best had never suspected the depth and power of that love of country which threw it into an agony of grief when the flag was here humbled, how should *they* conceive of it, who were wholly disjoined from them in sympathy? The whole land rose up, you remember, when the flag came down, as if inspired unconsciously by the breath of the Almighty, and the power of omnipotence. It was as when one pierces the banks of the Mississippi for a rivulet, and the whole raging stream plunges through with headlong course. There they calculated, and *mis*calculated!

And more than all, they miscalculated the bravery of men who have been trained under law, who are civilized, and hate personal brawls, who are so protected by society as to have dismissed all thought of self-defence, the whole force of whose life is turned to peaceful pursuits. These arrogant conspirators against government, with Chinese vanity, believed that they could blow away these self-respecting citizens, as chaff from the battle-field. Few of them are left alive to ponder their mistake!

Here, then, are the roots of this civil war. It was not a quarrel of wild beasts, it was an inflection of the strife of ages, between power and right, between ambition and equity. An armed band of pestilent conspirators sought the nation's life. Her children rose up and fought at every door, and room and hall, to thrust out the murderers, and save the house and household. It was not legitimately a war *between the common people* of the North and South. The war was set on by the ruling class, the aristocratic conspirators of the South. They suborned the common people with lies, with sophistries, with cruel deceits and slanders, to fight for secret objects which they abhorred, and against interests as dear to them as their own lives.

I charge the whole guilt of this war upon the ambitious, educated, plotting, political leaders of the South. (Applause.) They have shed this ocean of blood. They have desolated the South. They have poured poverty through all her towns and cities. They have bewildered the imagination of the people with phantasms, and led them to believe that they were fighting for their homes and liberty, whose homes were unthreatened, and whose liberty was in no jeopardy.

These arrogant instigators of civil war have renewed the plagues of Egypt, not that the oppressed might go free, but that the free might be oppressed. A day will come when God will reveal judgment, and arraign at his bar these mighty miscreants; and then every orphan that their bloody game has made, and every widow that sits sorrowing, and every maimed and wounded sufferer, and every bereaved heart in all the wide regions of this land, will rise up and come before the Lord to lay upon these chief culprits of modern history their awful witness. And from a thousand battle-fields shall rise up armies of airy witnesses, who, with the memory of their awful sufferings, shall confront these miscreants with shrieks of fierce accusation; and every pale and starved prisoner shall raise his skinny hand in judgment. Blood shall call out for vengeance, and tears shall plead for justice, and grief shall silently beckon, and love, heart-smitten, shall wail for justice. Good men and angels will cry out, "How long, oh Lord, how long, wilt thou not avenge?"

And, then, these guiltiest and most remorseless traitors, these high and cultured men with might and wisdom, used for the destruction of their country; these most accursed and detested of all criminals, that have drenched a continent in needless blood, and moved the foundations of their times with hideous crimes and cruelty, caught up in black clouds, full of voices of vengeance and lurid with punishment, shall be whirled aloft and plunged downward forever and forever in an endless retribution; while God shall say, "Thus shall it be to all who betray their country"; and all in heaven and upon the earth will say "Amen!" (Voices: Amen! Amen!)

But for the people misled, for the multitudes drafted and driven into this civil war, let not a trace of animosity remain. (Applause.) The moment the willing hand drops the musket, and they return to their allegiance, then stretch out your own honest right hand to greet them. Recall to them the old days of kindness. Our hearts wait for their redemption. All the resources of a renovated nation shall be applied to rebuild their prosperity, and smooth down the furrows of war.

[At this point in his oration, Mr. Beecher paused, and said, "I will thank the band to play an air, and you to get up that are sitting down, and you to sit down that have been standing: and I will sit down, too, and rest for a moment." When the band had ceased playing, he said: "We will now take our places again, and attend to our business," and then proceeded with his speaking.]

Has this long and weary period of strife been an unmingled evil? Has nothing been gained? Yes, much. This nation has attained to its manhood.

Among Indian customs is one which admits young men to the rank of warriors only after severe trials of hunger, fatigue, pain, endurance. They reach their station, not through years, but ordeals. Our nation has suffered, and now is strong.

The sentiment of loyalty and patriotism, next in importance to religion, has been rooted and grounded. We have something to be proud of, and pride helps love. Never so much as now did we love our country. (Great applause.)

But four such years of education in ideas, in the knowledge of political truth, in the lore of history, in the geography of our own country, almost every inch of which we have probed with the bayonet, have never passed before. There is half a hundred years' advance in four.

We *believed* in our institutions and principles before; but now we *know* their power. It is one thing to look upon artillery, and be sure that it is loaded; it is another thing to receive its discharge. (Laughter.) We believed in the hidden power stored in our institutions; we had never before seen this nation thundering like Mount Sinai at all those that worshipped the calf at the base of the mountain.

A people educated and moral are competent to all the exigencies of national life. A vote can govern better than a crown. We have proved it. (Applause.) A people intelligent and religious are strong in all economic elements. They are fitted for peace and competent to war. They are not easily inflamed; and, when justly incensed, not easily extinguished. They are patient in adversity, endure cheerfully needful burdens, tax themselves for real wants more royally than any prince would dare to tax his people. They pour forth, without stint, relief for the sufferings of war, and raise charity out of the realm of a dole, into a munificent duty of beneficence.

The habit of industry among free men prepares them to meet the exhaustion of war with increase of productiveness commensurate with the need that exists. Their habits of skill enable them at once to supply such armies as only freedom can muster, with arms and munitions such as only free industry can create. Free society is terrible in war, and afterwards repairs the mischief of war with a celerity almost as great as that with which the ocean heals the seams gashed in it by the keel of the plowing ship.

Free society is fruitful of military genius. It comes when called: when no longer needed, it falls back as waves do to the level of the common sea, that no wave may be greater than the undivided water. With proof of strength so great, yet in its infancy, we stand up among the nations of the world asking no privileges, asserting no rights, but quietly assuming our place, and determined to be second to none in the race of civilization and religion.

Of all nations, we are the most dangerous and the least to be feared. (Laughter and applause.) We need not expound the perils that wait upon enemies that assault us. They are sufficiently understood! (Laughter.) But we are not a dangerous people because we are warlike. All the arrogant attitudes of this nation, so offensive to foreign governments, were inspired by slavery, and under the administration of its minions. Our tastes, our habits, our interests and our principles, incline us to the arts of peace.

This nation was founded *by* the common people, *for* the common people. We are seeking to embody in public economy more liberty, with higher justice and virtue, than have been organized before. By the necessity of our doctrines, we are put in sympathy with the masses of men in all nations. It is not our business to subdue nations, but to augment the powers of the common people. The vulgar ambition of mere domination, as it belongs to universal human nature may tempt us; but it is withstood by the whole force of our principles, our habits, our precedents and our legends.

We acknowledge the obligation which our better political principles lay upon us to set an example more temperate, humane and just, than monarchical governments can. We will not suffer wrong, and still less will we inflict it upon other nations. Nor are we concerned that so many ignorant of our conflict, for the present, misconceive the reasons of our invincible military zeal. "Why contend," say they, "for a little territory that you do not need?" *Because it is ours!* (Laughter and applause.) Because it is the interest of every citizen to save it from becoming a fortress and refuge of iniquity. This nation is our house, and our fathers' house; and accursed be the man who will not defend it to the uttermost. (Applause.) More territory than we need? England, that is not large enough to be our pocket, (laughter,) may think that it is more than we need; but we are better judges of what we need than they are!

Shall a philanthropist say to a banker who defends himself against a robber, "Why do you need so much money?" But we will not reason with such questions. When any foreign nation willingly will divide their territory and give it cheerfully away, we will answer the question why we are fighting for territory! (Laughter.)

At present—for I pass to the consideration of benefits that accrue to the South in distinction from the rest of the nation—the South reaps only suffering; but good seed lies buried under the furrows of war, that peace will bring to harvest.

1. Deadly doctrines have been purged away in blood. The subtile poison of secession was a perpetual threat of revolution. The sword has ended that danger. That which reason had affirmed as a philosophy, the people have settled as a fact. Theory pronounces, "There can be no permanent government where each integral particle has liberty to fly off." Who would venture upon

a voyage on a ship, each plank and timber of which might withdraw at its pleasure? (Laughter and applause.) But the people have reasoned by the logic of the sword and of the ballot, and they have declared that States are inseparable parts of national government. They are not sovereign. State rights remain; but sovereignty is a right higher than all others; and that has been made into a common stock for the benefit of all. (Applause.) All further agitation is ended. This element must be cast out of political problems. Henceforth that poison will not rankle in the blood.

2. Another thing has been learned; the rights and duties of minorities. The people of the whole nation are of more authority than the people of any section. These United States are supreme over Northern, Western and Southern States. It ought not to have required the awful chastisement of this war to teach that a minority must submit the control of the nation's government to a majority. The army and navy have been good political schoolmasters. (Laughter and applause.) The lesson is learned. Not for many generations will it require further illustration.

3. No other lesson will be more fruitful of peace than the dispersion of those conceits of vanity, which, on either side, have clouded the recognition of the manly courage of all Americans. If it be a sign of manhood to be able to fight, then Americans are men. The North, certainly, are in no doubt whatever of the soldierly qualities of Southern men. Southern soldiers have learned that all latitudes breed courage on this continent. Courage is a passport to respect. The people of all the regions of this nation are likely hereafter to cherish a generous admiration of each other's prowess. The war has bred respect, and respect will breed affection, and affection peace and unity. (Applause.)

4. No other event of the war can fill an intelligent Southern man of candid nature with more surprise, than the revelation of the capacity, moral and military, of the black race. It is a revelation indeed. No people were ever less understood by those most familiar with them. They were said to be lazy, lying, impudent and cowardly wretches, driven by the whip alone to the tasks

needful to their own support, and the functions of civilization. They were said to be dangerous, blood-thirsty, liable to insurrection; but four years of tumultuous distress and war have rolled across the area inhabited by them, and I have yet to hear of one authentic instance of the misconduct of a colored man. They have been patient and gentle and docile, and full of faith and hope and piety; and when summoned to freedom they have emerged with all the signs and tokens that freedom will be to them what it was to be—the swaddling band that shall bring them to manhood. And after the Government honoring them as men, summoned them to the field, when once they were disciplined, and had learned the art of war, they have proved themselves to be not second to their white brethren in arms. And when the roll of men that have shed their blood is called in the other land, many and many a dusky face will rise, dark no more, when the light of eternal glory shall shine upon it from the throne of God.

5. The industry of the Southern States is regenerated, and now rests upon a basis that never fails to bring prosperity. Just now industry is collapsed; but it is not dead. It sleepeth. It is vital yet. It will spring like mown grass from the roots that need but showers and heat, and time to bring them forth. Though in many districts not a generation will see wanton wastes of self-invoked war repaired, and many portions may lapse again to wilderness; yet, in our life-time we shall see States, as a whole, raised to a prosperity, vital, wholesome and immovable.

6. The destruction of class interests, working with a religion, which tends towards true democracy in proportion, as it is pure and free, will create a new era of prosperity for the common laboring people of the South. Upon them has come the labor, the toil, and the loss of this war. They have fought blind-folded. They have fought for a class that sought their degradation, while they were made to believe that it was for their own homes and altars. Their leaders meant a supremacy which would not long have left them political liberty, save in name. But their leaders are swept away. The sword has been hungry for the ruling classes. It has sought them out with remorseless zeal. New

men are to rise up; new ideas are to bud and blossom; and there will be men with different ambition and altered policy.

7. Meanwhile, the South, no longer a land of plantations, but of farms; no longer tilled by slaves, but by freedmen, will find no hindrance to the spread of education. Schools will multiply. Books and papers will spread. Churches will bless every hamlet. There is a good day coming for the South. Through darkness, and tears, and blood she has sought it. It has been an unconscious *via dolorosa*. But, in the end, it will be worth all it has cost. Her institutions before were deadly. She nourished death in her bosom. The greater her secular prosperity, the more sure was her ruin. Every year of delay but made the change more terrible. Now, by an earthquake, the evil is shaken down. And her own historians, in a better day, shall write that from the day the sword cut off the cancer she began to find her health.

What, then, shall hinder the rebuilding of this republic? The evil spirit is cast out: why should not this nation cease to wander among tombs, cutting itself? Why should it not come, clothed, and in its right mind, to "sit at the feet of Jesus?" Is it feared that the Government will oppress the conquered States? What possible motive has the Government to narrow the base of that pyramid on which its own permanence stands?

Is it feared that the rights of the States will be withheld? The South is not more jealous of their State rights than the North. State rights, from the earliest colonial days, have been the peculiar pride and jealousy of New England. In every stage of national formation, it was peculiarly Northern, and not Southern, statesmen that guarded State rights as we were forming the Constitution. But, once united, the loyal States give up forever that which had been delegated to the National Government. And now, in the hour of victory, the loyal States do not mean to trench upon Southern States rights. They will not do it, or suffer it to be done. There is not to be one rule for high latitudes, and another for low. We take nothing from the Southern States that has not already been taken from Northern. The South shall have just those rights that every Eastern, every Middle, every Western State has—no more, no less.

We are not seeking our own aggrandizement by impoverishing the South. Its prosperity is an indispensable element of our own. We have shown, by all that we have suffered in war, how great is our estimate of the importance of the Southern States of this Union; and we will measure that estimate, now, in peace, by still greater exertions for their rebuilding.

Will reflecting men perceive, then, the wisdom of accepting established facts; and, with alacrity of enterprise, begin to retrieve the past?

Slavery cannot come back. It is the interest, therefore, of every man to hasten its end. Do you want more war? Are you not yet weary of contest? Will you gather up the unexploded fragments of this prodigious magazine of all mischief, and heap them up for continued explosion? Does not the South need peace? And, since free labor is inevitable, will you have it in its worst forms or its best? Shall it be ignorant, impertinent, indolent? or, shall it be educated, self-respecting, moral, and self-supporting? Will you have men as drudges, or will you have them as citizens? Since they have vindicated the Government, and cemented its foundation stones with their blood, may they not offer the tribute of their support to maintain its laws and its policy? It is better for religion; it is better for political integrity; it is better for industry; it is better for *money*—if you will have that ground motive—that you should educate the black man; and, by education, make him a citizen. (Applause.) They who refuse education to a black man, would turn the South into a vast poor-house, and labor into a pendulum, necessity vibrating between poverty and indolence.

From this pulpit of broken stone we speak forth our earnest greeting to all our land.

We offer to the President of these United States our solemn congratulations that God has sustained his life and health under the unparalleled burdens and sufferings of four bloody years, and permitted him to behold this auspicious consummation of that national unity for which he has waited with so much patience and fortitude, and for which he has labored with such disinterested wisdom. (Applause.)

To the members of the Government associated with him in the administration of perilous affairs in critical times; to the Senators and Representatives of the United States who have eagerly fashioned the instruments by which the popular will might express and enforce itself, we tender our grateful thanks. (Applause.)

To the officers and men of the army and navy, who have so faithfully, skillfully, and gloriously upheld their country's authority, by suffering, labor, and sublime courage, we offer here a tribute beyond the compass of words. (Great applause.)

Upon those true and faithful citizens, men and women, who have borne up with unflinching hope in the darkest hour, and covered the land with the labors of love and charity, we invoke the divinest blessing of Him whom they have so truly imitated. (Applause.)

But, chiefly to Thee, God of our fathers, we render thanksgiving and praise for that wondrous providence that has brought forth, from such a harvest of war, the seed of so much liberty and peace.

We invoke peace upon the North. Peace be to the West. Peace be upon the South.

In the name of God, we lift up our banner, and dedicate it to Peace, Union, and Liberty, now and forevermore. Amen. (Great applause.)

At the conclusion of the Address, the vast audience rose to their feet, and poured out their hearts in thankfulness, by singing:

7. The Doxology, to the tune of "Old Hundred."

"Praise God from whom all blessings flow!
Praise Him all creatures here below!
Praise Him above, ye heavenly host!
Praise Father, Son and holy Ghost!"

Never did a loftier enthusiasm inspire, and uplift the hearts of patriotic men, than when the stately, choral measures of this sublime ascription rose mightily, beyond the flag, beyond the stars, to the ear and heart of the Lord of Hosts!

But the exercise upon so significant and illustrious an occasion, would have been incomplete, without a devout recognition of that wisdom which had guided the national counsels; that goodness which had filled the cycle of four years past with blessing and progress; and that strong "right hand and holy arm," which had "gotten us the victory."

All heads were therefore reverently bowed, and all lips responded a fervent "Amen," as we joined in heart, with

8. The Closing Prayer and Benediction.

BY REV. R. S. STORRS, JR., D.D.

As this prayer was *read*, and withal was a rare production of appropriateness, comprehensiveness, earnest patriotism, lofty faith and fervid eloquence; it will gratify all our readers, to find it exactly transcribed in this work.

We append it here.

PRAYER.

Almighty God, our Heavenly Father, who wast, and art, and art to come, the Eternal Ruler of worlds and men, having Thy glory above the heavens, Holy and Reverend is Thy Name. Before Thy throne we humbly bow, confessing our sins, and seeking the continual aids of Thy grace. Unto Thee we render our joyful thanks, that Thou hast been pleased to reveal Thyself to us, through Thy Son and Thy Spirit, as ready to hear and answer prayer.

Thine, oh Lord! are power and majesty; glory and victory are Thine. We worship and adore Thee for Thine infinite holiness, for Thy wisdom and might, for Thy clemency and goodness, and for Thine unsearchable love to mankind. We adore Thee for Thine immutable sovereignty, in Providence and in grace; that Thou doest Thy pleasure in the armies of Heaven, and dost sweetly ordain and irresistibly establish Thy counsel in the earth; and that all Thy works are done in truth. And assembled before Thee in these public solemnities, on a day, and in a scene, consecrated by memories of sorrow and fidelity, of sacrifice and of victory, we give Thee especial thanks for all Thy goodness to us as a people; most of all in the bloody and terrible years through which of late Thou hast caused us to pass. We thank Thee for the leaders whom Thou hast raised up for us, in the Cabinet and the Field; for their wisdom in council, for their religious consecration and trust; for their valor, and skill, and fortitude in war. We thank Thee for the successes with which thou hast been pleased to crown our arms, on the land and the sea; for the signal victories which of late we have gotten, not by our skill and will alone, but by the might of Him, who hath helped us; and for the discomfiture of the plans of our enemies.

We mourn before Thee, for the thousands who have fallen, our beauty and strength, upon our high places. But we bless Thee and praise Thee, that their suffering and death have not been in vain, and that from their graves, the Nation which they loved hath drawn, by Thy grace, a nobler life; that its unity is maintained; that its revered institutions are preserved; that the shame and curse of oppression are removed from it; that its throne henceforth is established in righteousness; and that on it there hang their memorable names, as a thousand bucklers, all shields of mighty men.

And now, we pray Thee, oh! Lord of Hosts, who was the God of our fathers aforetime, and in whose name we have set up our banners, that the flag now raised anew above these walls, by the hand of Thy servant, may never be lowered before the onset of foreign war; before the more deadly assault of treason; that being upheld and advanced by Thee, whose counsel is infinite, and whose right hand is glorious in power, it may shine forever on the front of our land, the symbol of Christian liberty and law, of peace, and hope, and universal well being.

With Thy merciful favor behold, we beseech Thee, and plenteously bless, Thy servant, the President of these United States, and all who are, in any station associated with him, in the conduct of the government, the enactment or the administration of law. Instruct and direct them by Thy Holy Spirit, and endue them with Thy grace; that as mortal, yet immortal, accountable to History and responsible to Thee, they may plan with prudence, may labor with diligence, may wait with constant hope and faith, and may see Thy work always prospering in their hand.

Bless those who are at the head of our armies and navies, and those in every rank of command. Make them to be strong and of a good courage; ride upon the heavens in their help, O most High; shelter their heads in the day of battle; make them merciful and humane, as well as valiant and wise, and preserve them hereafter, as Thou hast hitherto, from undue exultation in the hour of victory.

Bless those who serve, with faithful hearts, in whatever place, in our armies and navies. Teach their hands to war, and their fingers to fight, yet let them ever be mindful of Thee, and may they live to receive the reward of all their perils in the gratitude of their country, and in Thy smile.

Remember those who are sick and wounded, in camp and hospital, and those who are prisoners afar from home. Grant them speedy healing, and quick release; and may they have succor in their feebleness and pain, and solace and society in their solitude and want, through Thy benediction.

Remember those who have been our enemies, and turn their hearts from wrath and war, to love and peace. Let the desolations that have come on them suffice, and unite them with us in ties of a better brotherhood than of old; that the cities, and homes, and happiness they have lost may be more than replaced in the long prosperity they shall hereafter know.

Grant Thy Fatherly blessing unto all this nation, founded in faith, devoted to Thee in its early baptism of fire and blood, and now again signally saved by Thy hand. Thou has given to it the precious fruits brought forth by the sun, and the precious things put forth by the moon, the chief things of the ancient mountains, and the precious things of the lasting hills. May the good will of Him that dwelt in the bush, be also its inheritance, and let Thy blessing come upon its head; that being not only restored but renewed, being purified in its spirit and perfected for Thy service, by the sorrows and the wonders through which it hath been led, it may be a nation forevermore to Thine honor and praise; the kingdom of Thy favor, the people and the nation of Thy right hand. So hasten through it the coming of the day, when all the kingdoms shall be at last the kingdoms of Thy Son, and when the kindreds and tribes of the earth, knit together in love, shall learn and practice war no more.

And now, O God, our Heavenly Father, help us who are here assembled before Thee, and who never again shall be here assembled before Thee, and who never again shall be so assembled, until we stand before Thy bar to consecrate ourselves afresh, on this historic day to the welfare of our land; to the cause, and the cross, and the truth of our Lord; that we may live evermore to Thy glory, may walk in Thy light, may die at last in thy perfect peace, and may arise to our rest in the bosom of Thy love.

We offer all these our praises and thanksgivings, and ask all these inestimable gifts, only in His most worthy name, who loved us, and sought us, and gave Himself for us, even unto the bitter death upon the Cross, and unto whom, with Thee, O Father! and the Holy Ghost, shall be honor and praise, and dominion and power, henceforth and forever, world without end. Amen.

The prayer being ended with the Benediction, the grand ceremonial, which must ever live upon the annals of our country's history was concluded. But for a while the assemblage seemed riveted to the spot. During certain portions of the ceremony, a strange absence of demonstrative enthusiasm had been observed. *Once*, when the flag went up, it was irrepressible, tumultuous and overmastering. At other times, it was only moderate, and seemed inadequate to the suggestions and demands of the occasion. No other solution can be given of this, than the natural difficulty in expressing enthusiasm according to a programme; or that the feeling of the participants was too deep, and pervasive and solemn, for noisy demonstration.

But at the close of the services, once more it broke forth, and a vigorous "*twice three*," was given for the old flag, three more for Gen. Anderson, as many for President Lincoln, another round for Gen. Gilmore, Mr. Beecher, and other celebrities; and the historic scene was over; the power of the United States over the waters of Charleston Harbor, and the soil of South Carolina, was vindicated; and the banner of the Republic, soon to be restored, was left floating at the peak, never to be displaced again by rebellious hands, while the names of Washington and Lincoln linger in the memory of mankind.

The crowd now slowly dispersed about the fort, surveying the surrounding scenery from the parapet, exploring the casemates and bomb-proofs where many of the large guns still remain; rumaging amidst the debris for relics, unearthing great pieces of shell or canister shot, rusty bits of iron, bolts and screws which they carried about until weary, and then threw away, for some less ponderous souvenir; plucking leaves and flowers from the speakers' stand, indulging in general hand shaking with the military celebrities upon the platform, recognizing old acquaintances, and waiting for the steamboats and transports to come up to the dock, that they might reëmbark for the city.

Meanwhile the "Planter," whose load of contrabands, for some as yet unexplained reason, had not been permitted to land and witness the ceremonies within the fort, had been left aground at the landing, by the falling tide. No effort of her own could set her afloat. Much confusion and delay ensued. The passengers of the "Oceanus," were compelled to cross the decks of the "Planter," the "Delaware," and the "Robert Coit," to reach the "Golden Gate."

In passing from the "Planter" to the "Delaware," the crowd became very dense and impatient. The bow of the former lay hard against the side of the latter. It was necessary to step from the upper deck of the one, which converged to a point, upon the deck of the other. A part of the railing of the "Planter," was broken away at the right, and nothing was between the crowding men and women, and the water below, except the high upper deck upon which we stood. Those behind pressed hard upon those in advance. Warning voices were heard saying that the weak deck would give away. Many were crowded to the very verge. There was real danger of some being pushed into the water. One by one, and very slowly at that, the people were handed over the narrow pass. And we record these circumstances thus minutely, because it was regarded as a noteworthy Providence, that not the slightest accident befel any person, who made the transit. Furthermore it may be added, that no casualty whatever occurred throughout the entire day, to mar the enjoyment and harmony of the occasion.

The living freight, at last being duly shipped, the "Golden Gate" and the "Delaware," now attached their cables to the "Planter," and drew her from her moorings of mud. Once detached, she seemed irresistible. Her strong wheels conducted themselves as though desirous of being avenged for their temporary disgrace. Robert Small again stood on the top of the wheelhouse, and shouted his commands. A little less zeal and more discretion on the part of this colored captain, would have prevented a momentary fright for our ladies. For, failing to give the signal for reversing in time, he allowed his dun-colored craft to come crashing into our port wheel-house, making both the splinters and the color fly. However, no serious damage was done by the colision. The "Planter" with its motley crew, and a few of our own party who had failed to reach the "Golden Gate," among whom we noticed our Honorable Mayor of Brooklyn, slowly wheeled, and then gallantly led the van of all the vessels, on the return to the city of Charleston.

After sundry mysterious backings and circuits of our

own craft around the fort, at length she turned her bow towards the spires of the city, and soon we were once more on board the "Oceanus," partaking of an excellent supper, for which long fasting had given the keenest relish.

As the sun went down over the waters of the western sea, the echoes which had slumbered since the salute to the risen flag, were again awakened by the thunder of cannon from all the shipping.

In the evening, at 8 o'clock, we were summoned to the decks, to witness a most unique and beautiful illumination, as the closing demonstration of the day. At a given signal from the flag-ship, every man-of-war, transport and monitor in the harbor, became a skeleton pyramid of flame. Lanterns thickly slung to the rigging and culminating at the top of the mainmast, flashed out a starry light or line of lights, reduplicated by reflection in the water, while on the decks the most brilliant Gregorian fires of red, white, blue, green, pink, purple and gold, were lighted, whose columns of smoke, rolling lazily upward and illuminated respectively by their own peculiar flame, presented a spectacle of almost dazzling beauty. Rockets of great power and towering flight, screamed skyward from every deck, and bursting with a muffled sound, dissolved into various gorgeous tints, dropped gently downward, and quenched their splendor in the tide.

Hark! the boom of a single gun from the flag-ship. Presto! change! In a moment the lights are extinguished, the lanterns run down, the rockets, blue lights, and Gregorian fires have ceased their pyrotechnics, and again silence and darkness lap their wings over the waters of the Bay.

Thus ended the celebration of April 14th, 1865, the day of the flag's resurrection, the day of swelling patriotic joy for all the leal and loyal; the day for which the North has prayed, fought, bled and suffered; the day which admonishes all the nations; the day which posterity will celebrate, and for which they will ever give glory to Almighty God.

We find in the correspondence of the "Tribune," from the pen of Mr. A. M. Powell, the following brief notice of the reception at Gen. Hatch's headquarters in the evening.

"In the evening, Gen. Hatch gave a ball, which was largely attended, at the former palatial residence of Col. Ash. It was just four years previous that Col. Ash himself gave a grand ball at the same place, in honor of the fall of Sumter. Some of those in attendance as waiters upon the ball given by Gen. Hatch, now free men and women, were at the ball four years previous as the slaves of Col. Ash. Their comments, in contrasting the people assembled upon the two occasions, were highly favorable to those at the North, especially the northern ladies."

Many of the passengers, not in attendance upon the ball, were deeply interested in the narrations of Capt. Robert Small, who paid a visit to our steamer, during

6

the evening. He is a stoutly built man, of little more than medium height, of intelligent countenance, ready speech, entire self-possession, and considerable humor. He described minutely his experience four years ago; as his plans were delayed and thwarted by the cowardice of his associates, as at length he resolved to succeed or die in the attempt, as he cut the moorings of his vessel, and lowered them by strings into the water, that no splash might awaken the sentry; as he moved slowly along the river, and took on board his own wife and children, with those of his companions; as he guided the steamer through the vessels in the harbor, to the walls of Fort Sumter, at 3 o'clock in the morning, receiving there no notice; as weary of waiting, at length he steamed, with many a narrow escape from detection, past all the rebel batteries, and at last delivered his vessel, and all on board, to the U. S. blockading fleet, outside of the bar.

For more than an hour he submitted to the most rigid catechising, by the curious passengers, answering every question with surprising intelligence, and frequently with genuine wit of repartee.

He has the least possible faith in the loyalty of Gov. Aiken, or any of those who are returning to take the oath of allegiance. The Government estimated the value of the "Planter" at $9,000, of which he received one half. He is now in independent circumstances, and is regarded by all the other negroes as immensely rich, and decidedly "the smartest *cullud* man in Souf Car'lina."

At an unexpectedly early hour, some of the guests of General Hatch returned to the boat. Upon being asked the reason, they replied that their hearts were not there, "that they had been disturbed throughout the evening, by certain strange presentiments and foreshadowings of evil."

How little recked they of that cloud of cimmerian darkness, in which a more northern sun had but just gone down; of the scene transpiring in the nation's Capital, at the very hour when the buoyant ones in the saloons of Rebel chiefs, were "chasing the glowing hours with flying feet?"

But we would not lift the curtain a moment too soon.

The wearied dancers returned to the steamer, at the spectral hours; the lights burned low; the cabins were still; and all, in "sleep's serene oblivion," were waiting for the morrow.

CHAPTER VI.

It had been announced that the "Oceanus" would sail Saturday morning, at 10 o'clock, but a universal desire to see more of the city, and attend the "Freedmen's meeting," at Zion's Church, secured a postponement of the hour to 5 o'clock P. M., precisely. The day was therefore at the disposal of the company.

Glad of this extension of time, they were scattered, after breakfast, in every direction about the city, to finish their explorations. A few, whose tastes led them in that direction, went up to the mansion of Gov. Aiken, which notorious individual they found quite hospitable and communicative. As it would be impossible to describe *all* that was seen by our curious party of two hundred, we shall give the results of our own explorations, and the additional matter which has been kindly transmitted for our use in this volume.

Entering first the old "State Bank of South Carolina," we found it utterly ruined by fire, and the effect of shells. The rooms were wholly denuded; the charred rafters and sleepers everywhere protruding; the floors strewed with bank papers of every description, half burned and covered with dust and cinders. A glance

THE POST OFFICE.

at one room was sufficient, for all were in like condition. The Bank of Charleston, which we next visited, is much less injured and ravaged. Originally it was a much finer structure.

The marble-topped desks and counters remain, and are occupied by our officers, who make the bank a business dépôt. A gentlemanly official, lighting a candle, conducted our party into the vault, a room about 10 by 15 feet, lined on three sides, with pigeon holes, and carpeted now with worthless paper rubbish. The "Director's Room," handsomely frescoed and furnished, was in the possession of a U. S. officer. The rooms upon the second floor, were piled knee-deep with old bank accounts, notes, bills of exchange, papers of every description, and of the least possible intrinsic value. Here the mania for "relics" ran high. Dozens of curiosity-hunters were bending over them on hands and knees, untying old yellow and dusty bundles, selecting ancient and curious documents, and duly bestowing them in the voluminous depths of coat pockets, or carrying them off tenderly under the arm. Occasionally could be heard, "ah! here's a prize! only look! 1730, 1776," etc.

Enough of these valuable acquisitions were brought home to comfortably stock "No. 25 Ann St."

The old City Hall we found to be the rendezvous of the regiments which are now on guard in the city. Muskets were stacked before it and within it; patrols walked measuredly back and forth, while the "boys" off duty were asleep upon the benches and floors within. This building was in the same general condition of those before described, everything indicating that the Rebels went out in haste and by flight.

Precisely the same may be said of the Court-House, on the opposite corner of the street, never an imposing building, and now sacked, gloomy and desolate.

Upon the corner diagonally from the City Hall, stands the Guard-House, before which negro sentinels were pacing, with bayonets fixed. Entering here we found a number of contrabands in the large lower room, and boys of every size, with a few middle-aged men, all exceedingly ragged, but apparently very happy. In one corner, two youngsters were shuffling a pack of dirty cards. Mr. Wm. B. Bradbury, asked them, as they gathered curiously around, to sing some of their regular old plantation songs—or the melodies which they use in their "quarters." Accordingly they went through with several of their strange, hum-drum, droning airs, ringing the changes upon particular words or phrases, varying the melody by only three or four notes, and producing a very wierd effect. Sometimes they ended these monotonous chantings with a "shout," or accompanied them with a "break-down" dance. As they sang, Mr. Bradbury took down hurriedly the notes upon a slip of paper, and may hereafter give them greater publicity, as a curiosity of plantation melody.

One of the bystanders said:

"Boys do you know the John Brown song?"

"Oh! yas, Massa, we know John Brown!"

"Well, give it to us now!"

Then they broke forth:

> "John Brown's body lies a mouldering in the grave, etc.
> But his soul am marching *home*."

"Do you know the second verse, boys?"

"Yas! yas! we know de second verse too"—and they sang,

> "We'll hang Jeff Davis to a sour apple tree!
> We'll hang Jeff Davis to a sour apple tree!
> We'll hang Jeff Davis to a sour apple tree!
> *On Canaan's happy shore!*"

So simple and ludicrous, is the admixture of ideas in the minds of these untutored Africans! In their guiltless ignorance, they see no reason why "Canaan's happy shore," may not be an excellent place for an execution. And upon the principle of aggravation, why might it not, were it possible! Why might not the the most conscienceless and deepest dyed criminal which the nineteenth century has produced, fitly be hanged, where his last glance beyond the lightning hempen cord might be, at the "sweet fields dressed in living green," the "tree of everlasting life," the "golden streets," and the blissful choirs of the heavenly country, from which his towering and unrepented wickedness have forever debarred him? Underlying the thoughtless utterance of the manumitted slave, may be found some true philosophy.

Many of these simple-hearted, yet natively religious black men, having never heard the "Yankees" mentioned by their masters, except coupled with a profane prefix, have been praying for years with the most unctuous fervor, "O Lord! bress, we beseech Thee, and speedily bring along de comin' of de "*dam* Yankees."

And the Lord has heard them. Now the beings so long oppressed and degraded, seem to be living in the single idea that they are *free.* That thought has possessed them night and day, year after year, and now that freedom has come, can any wonder that it is difficult for them to realize it, and rise, at once, to the full understanding, not only of the privileges which it confers, but of the duties which it makes imperative? Their faith in their coming deliverance, has never wavered. One old colored exhorter, thus expressed it: "I know dat we was to be free, dat the day would come, when de Lord willed it, and I pray for it. I wait wid patience, for I know when de Lord's time did come, he would raise up a man, as he raised Moses, to deliber de people."

It has been asserted that the slaves were treated with so much kindness, that they would be unwilling to leave their masters for freedom.

A touching incident was related, which bears upon this point and may undoubtedly be accepted as representatives of almost the entire class.

A master was expressing surprise to his slave, a man of middle age, that he should be willing to leave him, "Have I not always treated you well, fed, clothed and cared for you. Do you really want to be free, and your own master!"

"Oh mas'r," replied the slave, "if you could only hab seen my *knees* for dese last seben years, how I'se prayed and prayed for freedom, you neber ax dat question."

All the streets along which we passed were alive with negroes, men, women, boys and girls, from the fine looking octoroons and whiter damsels, from fourteen to twenty years of age, dressed in clean, well-starched gowns of calico, and bonnets of modern style, to the elder women with fancy turbans; from the little ragged, sooty "piccaninnies," rolling in the sand, or playing on the sidewalk, to the decrepit, grey-headed old men, sitting doubled up on the curb-stone or steps of the stores, all watching eagerly the new crowd of passers by. The amount of "shinplasters," given to these people, by the passengers of the "Oceanus," cannot ever be conjectured, but it was a matter of devout desire, that evening, that the steamer would sail at once, lest a day or two longer in the city, would leave our company with fearfully gaunt portmonaies. Five of the slaves of Gov. Aiken, were huddled in a doorway—a father and mother, with three children—and five more ignorant, bedraggled and wretched creatures, it would be difficult to find.

One good-looking, intelligent negress, ran after us as we passed, and touching our companion upon the arm, exclamed:

"Oh! ain't you Mr. Ames, sir?"

Our good-natured fellow passenger, blandly ignored any title to that brief patronymic.

"I thought it must be, you look so much like dat gemman."

We fell into conversation with her.

"Aunty," said we, you are free!"

"Oh sar," she cried, striking her hands frequently together, "free as de birds of de air, bress de Lord!"

"Well," we responded, you won't call any man 'massa,' again, will you?"

Oh, *No sah, no sah!* It doesn't seem as if I *could* make up my mouf to say 'massa,' again to any man."

"Aunty, how old are you!"

"Don't know precisely, sah! 'spect I'm nearly fifty years old."

"How many children have you?"

"I've had thirteen, sah! my first child was born when I was fourteen years old."

"Have you a husband!"

"Yes, sah! *dar's* my ole man," pointing to a hale and hearty negro, sitting upon the door-stone, a few steps off. "Come along here, John, want to 'duce ye to dese yer Northern gemman!" And John came up, with grinning visage, and rolling gait, and submitted to the operation of "*ducing*," which being accomplished, he modestly retired, and left the colloquy to his more communicative, if not better half.

We passed on towards the citadel and common. On every block were marks of ruin and desertion still. A very few stores were open, with the most meagre stock of the simplest articles, and a lamentable paucity of purchasers. But the most of the stores were abandoned, the shells having made them untenable. The signs remain, and many a familiar name and firm were recognized. One gentlemen of our party, standing at the crossing of the streets, pointed out to us the signs of *eleven* firms "which" said he "owe us money in sums from one thousand to eleven thousand dollars"—Another gentleman looking obliquely down Broad street, exclaimed "Ah, there's a firm that owes me over a thousand dollars!"

The slave-mart attracted much attention—the veritable pens in which families were kept, and at the auction block, separated forever. The day of traffic in human flesh is past—the dreadful marts are closed, and the wail of their agonized victims will never more be heard in the streets of Charleston.

We were shown also the jail, with its dark dungeons and instruments of torture for refractory slaves! another obsolete institution in the city, and destined to become so throughout every State of the free Republic.

Pausing here for a few moments in this narration, we turn to speak of the great meetings held on "Citadel Square" and in "Zion's Church." At an early hour the colored people had began to assemble about the stands erected for the speakers. The colored public school children met at the school houses and marched in procession, led by Superintendent Redpath, to the square.

While waiting for the speakers to arrive, Major Delaney, (colored,) of General Saxton's staff, made an address to the crowd.

Arrival of Wm. Lloyd Garrison.

Just before 10 o'clock, the surging and cheering of the vast throng announced the arrival of Mr. Garrison. It was impossible to repress the enthusiasm of that crowd of freemen. Not content with deafening shouts, they pressed towards their illustrious friend, and bore him on their shoulders to the speaker's stand. At sight of this demonstration, Major Delaney remarked that "this day should be the resurrection of John C. Calhoun."

A single incident related by one of our passengers, Mr. J. L. Leonard, of Lowville, N. Y., will illustrate the interest which absorbed the freedmen, as these scenes were being enacted. He says:

"You remember that the Citadel Square was filled with colored people on the 15th of April, and the children, hundreds in number, from the colored schools, were marching in procession, singing "John Brown" and other songs. As I passed through the crowd, I saw an old negro, who must have been over seventy years of age, sitting on the low wall, and noticing that he had a wooden leg, I went up and inquired of him how he lost his leg. He attempted to answer, but was too much absorbed in the spectacle before him to reply, and as the tears rolled down his face, he exclaimed 'My God! My God! what a sight!' 'Peace! Peace!' and then hearing the report of a fire-arm, he started up in alarm, asking, 'What's that!' his thoughts evidently going back to former days. He immediately turned his attention again to the children, and was so completely overcome that it was some time before he could reply to my question. The intense interest manifested by this poor old man made a strong impression upon me, and I have often thought of it since as an illustration of the peculiar emotional nature of that race, of which I had often heard, but which I had never before witnessed."

As it was not possible for Senator Wilson to speak in the open air, an adjournment was immediately made to Zion's Church. It is estimated that 3,000 freedmen crowded themselves within its walls.

Upon the platform were to be seen the Hon. Henry Wilson, William Lloyd Garrison, George Thompson, General Saxton, Theodore Tilton, Judge Kelly, of Penn., Dr. J. Leavitt, and others. In front of the platform was a large number of army and navy officers, and visitors, including several ladies.

When all were seated, a freedman, named Samuel Dickerson, accompanied by his two daughters, bearing a beautiful wreath of flowers, advanced to the pulpit, and addressing Mr. Garrison, said:

Sir—It is with pleasure that is inexpressible that I welcome you here among us, the long, the steadfast friend of the poor, downtrodden slave. Sir, I have read of you. I have read of the mighty labors you have had for the consummation of this glorious object. Here you see stand before you your handiwork. These children were robbed from me, and I stood desolate. Many a night I pressed a sleepless pillow from the time I returned to my couch until the close of the morning. I lost a dear wife, and after her death that little one, who is the counterpart of her mother's countenance, was taken from me. I appealed for her with all the love and reason of a father. The rejection came forth in these words: "Annoy me not, or I will sell them off to another State." I thank God that through your instrumentality, under the folds of that glorious flag which treason tried to triumph, you have restored them to me. And I tell you it is not this heart alone, but there are mothers, there are fathers, there are sisters, and there are brothers, the pulsation of whose hearts are unimaginable. The greeting that they would give you, Sir, it is almost impossible for me to express; but simply, Sir, we welcome and look upon you as our saviour. We thank you for what you have done for us. Take this wreath from these children, and when you go home, never mind how faded they may be, preserve them, encase them, and keep them as a token of affection from one who has loved and lived. (Cheers.)

Mr. Garrison, in reply, spoke as follows:

My Dear Friend—I have no language to express the feelings of my heart on listening to your kind and strengthening words, on receiving these beautiful tokens of your gratitude, and on looking into the faces of this vast multitude, now happily liberated from the galling fetters of slavery. Let me say at the outset: "Not unto us, not unto us, but unto God be all the glory" for what has been done in regard to your emancipation. I have been actually engaged in this work for almost forty years—for I began when I was quite young to plead the cause of the enslaved in this country. But I never expected to look you in the face, never supposed you would hear of anything I might do in your behalf. I knew only one thing—all that I wanted to know—that you were a grievously oppressed people; and that, on every consideration of justice, humanity, and right, you were entitled to immediate and unconditional freedom.

I hate slavery as I hate nothing else in this world. It is not only a crime, but the sum of all criminality; not only a sin, but the sin of sins against Almighty God. I cannot be at peace with it at any time, to any extent, under any circumstances. That I have been permitted to witness its overthrow calls for expressions of devout thanksgiving to heaven. It was not on account of your complexion or race, as a people, that I espoused your cause, but because you were the children of a common Father, created in the same divine image, having the same inalienable rights, and as much entitled to liberty as the proudest slaveholder that ever walked the earth.

For many a year I have been an outlaw at the South for your sakes, and a large price was set upon my head, simply because I endeavored to remember those in bonds as bound with them. Yes—God is my witness!—I have faithfully tried, in the face of the fiercest opposition, and under the most depressing circumstances, to make your cause my cause; my wife and children your wives and children, subjected to the same outrage and degradation; myself on the same auction-block, to be sold to the highest bidder. Thank God, this day you are free! (Great cheering.) And be resolved that, once free, you will be free forever. No—not one of you ever will, ever can consent again to become a bondman. Liberty or death, but never slavery. (Cheers.)

It gives me joy to assure you, that the American Government will stand by you to establish your freedom against whatever claims your former masters may bring. The time was when it gave no protection, but was on the side of the oppressor, where there was power. Now all is changed! Once, I could not feel any gladness at the sight of the American flag, because it was stained with your blood, and under it four millions of slaves were daily driven to unrequited labor. Now, it floats, purged of its gory stain; it symbolizes freedom for all, without distinction of race or color. The Government has its hold upon the throat of the monster Slavery, and is strangling the life out of it.

In conclusion, I thank you, my friend, for your affecting and grateful address, and for these handsome tokens of our Heavenly Father's wisdom and goodness, and will try to preserve them in accordance with your wishes. O, be assured, I never doubted that I had the gratitude and affection of the entire colored population of the United States, even though personally unknown to so many of them; because I knew that upon me heavily rested the wrath and hatred of your cruel oppressors. I was sure, therefore, if I had them against me, I had you with me. (Applause.) But, as it is now time to organize this meeting, it will not be proper for me to go on with these remarks any further, except to say that, long as I have labored in your behalf, while God gives me reason and strength I shall demand for you everything I claim for the whitest of the white in this country. (Great cheering.)

Major General SAXTON rose to introduce Senator WILSON, and was greeted with three cheers. Gen. SAXTON said:

MY FRIENDS—I did not want you to cheer for me to-day. There are soldiers in your cause here whose hats I am not worthy to hold, for they have been a great while in it. It is my happiness to-day to introduce to you an honored Senator from a noble State; my own loved native State, Massachusetts; one who through a long, able, consistent and brilliant career in the councils of the nation, has fought and borne his testimony against the living wickedness of human slavery; and when, in the future of your emancipated, regenerate and regenerating race, you shall read the record of its downfall, on the pages of its history shall shine brightly the name of Henry Wilson, of Massachusetts. (Cheers.)

MR. GARRISON—I wish to add one word more. I am delighted to find so strong a representation from Massachusetts in South Carolina. Of all the States in the Union, it is to her credit that she has always been the most hated and feared by the slaveholding South, for her anti-slavery spirit and tendencies. Senator Wilson has ably and faithfully sustained her reputation, in this particular, in Congress, for several years past; and for a much longer period has been your fearless friend and advocate. In the days of its deepest darkness and greatest perils, he unflinchingly supported your cause, which has been greatly advanced by his example and testimony. His life (as well as Mr. Sumner's) has been continually imperilled in the national capital; so that, from session to session, it has been uncertain whether he would ever be permitted to see his family and constituents again. He has fought a good fight, and deserves to be crowned with laurels. He began his career as a humble mechanic—one of the "mud sills," of whom some of you may perhaps have heard. He has, by his own merits, worked his way up to almost the highest station in the land, and is now one of the most esteemed and justly honored of our public men. Join with me in exclaiming, God bless Henry Wilson, of Massachusetts! (Cheers.)

Senator Wilson rose amid cheering, and after it had subsided said:

Men, Women and Freedmen of Charleston, and of South Carolina, and of the United States—This is the proudest day of my life. To stand here on the soil of South Carolina, in the home of the rebellion, on the platform with the great anti-slavery hero of our country, William Lloyd Garrison, and before the freedmen of the city of Charleston! (Great cheering.) For twenty-nine years in private life and in public life, at all times and on all occasions, I have spoken against slavery, voted against slavery, and in favor of the freedom of every man that breathes God's air or walks his earth. And to-day, standing here in South Carolina, I feel that the slave power we have fought so long is under my heel; (cheers)—and that men and women held in bondage for so long are free forevermore. You have no masters now. (Cheers.) You know no master but Almighty God. (Cheers.) Slave is no more written on your foreheads. Allow no man hereafter to call you a slave. Spread it abroad all over South Carolina, that the black men of South Carolina know no master now, and that they are slaves no more forever. (Great cheering.) Abraham Lincoln, President of the United States, (tremendous cheering and waving of hats, etc.) with twenty-five millions of freemen by his side, and seven hundred thousand bayonets behind him, has decreed it, and it will stand while the world stands, that the men and women of South Carolina can never more be slaves. They have robbed your cradles; they have sold your children; they have separated husband and wife, father and mother and child. (Cries of yes! yes! yes!) They shall separate you no more. (Hallelujah! Bless the Lord!) Let them understand it. Here to-day I proclaim it. I want the proud and haughty chivalry of South Carolina, whom I have met in the Congress of the United States to know it; I want them one and all to hear me to-day, and understand what I say, that the black men and the black women of South Carolina are as free as they are; and further, that they are loyal to the flag of the country, while they are false and traitorous. (Cheers.) Let them understand, too, that we, the people of the United States, and the Government of the United States, have more respect for a loyal black man than for a South Carolina white traitor.

Now I want you to understand these things. I want you to walk the soil of South Carolina with your foreheads to the skies, proud and erect, conscious that you are freemen, and that you owe your obligations, not to the master of the palace, but to the lowest of your nation, and to the God of heaven. (Cheers.)

And now, understanding that being your position, a position in which you are placed by the Government of the United States, a position in which you will be backed by the bayonets of the Government of the United States, if it ever be necessary to maintain your freedom—standing in this position, forever free, you and thousands who come after you, remember, oh, remember, the sacrifices that have been made for your freedom, and be worthy of the freedom that has come to you! (Cheers.) I know you will be.

Through these four years of bloody war, you have been always loyal to the old flag of the country. You have never betrayed your country; you have never betrayed the Union soldiers fighting the battles of the country. You have guided them, you have cheered them, you have protected them all through the country, and you have proved yourselves worthy the great occasion in which you are placed by the slaveholders' rebellion. You saw, four years ago, the flag of your country struck down from Sumter—yesterday you saw the old flag go up again. All its stars gleam now with a brighter lustre. You know now what the old flag means; that it means liberty to every man and woman in the country. (Cheers.)

You have been patient, you have endured, you have trusted in God for your liberties, and in your country; and the God of our fathers has blessed our country, and blessed you; and now you are here, the country is saved, the great army that carried the arms of this rebellion has surrendered to Gen. Grant. (Great cheers.) The long, dreary and chilly night of slavery has passed away forevermore. (Amen, Amen, Amen.) and the star of liberty casts its broad beams upon you to-day. Now your duties commence with your liberties. Remember that you are to be obedient, faithful, true, and loyal to the country forevermore. (Cheers and cries of yes! yes! yes!) Remember, too, that you are to educate your children; that you are to improve their condition; that you are to make a brighter future to them than the past has been to you. Remember that you are to be industrious; that freedom does not mean that you must not work, but it means that when you do work, you shall have pay for it to carry home to your wives, and the children of your love. Remember that liberty means the liberty to work for yourselves, to have the fruits of it to better your own condition, and improve the condition of your children. Respect yourselves. Feel and go about on earth conscious that you are freemen. Walk like freemen. Bow and cringe to nobody on earth. Be kind and humane to each other, always serving each other when you can. Be courteous and gentlemanly to everybody on earth, black and white. (Cheers.) But let those men who have held the lash over you for so many years; let the men who plunged the nation into a sea of fire and blood, let them understand that we have buried a quarter of a million of brave men to save our liberty and maintain yours.

Let it be understood, while the names of those heroes sound in our ears, that we have resolved that it is written on the leaves of our Bibles, and sworn on bended knee, that the United States of America shall be one nation, and a free nation forever. (Great cheering.)

You have helped us to fight our battles. You have taken your muskets, you have stood by the old flag, you have given us your prayers, you have had your heart's desire fulfilled. We have triumphed, and in our triumph we want all to stand up and rejoice together.

I want every man and every woman to understand here that every neglect of duty, every failure to be industrious, to be economical, to take care of your families, to support yourselves, to secure the education of your children; all these things will be put in our faces as a reproach, and your old masters will point you out and say, "We told you so." We have said for more than thirty years you were fit for liberty. We have maintained it amid obloquy and reproach, and in the halls of Congress were made a by-word. Now your masters have plunged the country into war. We have beaten them; we have whipped them; their power is broken, and it is lost forever. (Great cheering.) Now the great lesson is for you in the future to prove that we were right; to prove that you were worthy of all liberty and power yourselves. As you have used the bayonet, prepare yourselves for the future so that you can use the ballot in the cause we have maintained. (Great cheering.)

I see around me true and noble men who have come to see you in South Carolina. I know you will be glad to see and hear them, for they will speak to-day as they have spoken far away when the task-master stood over you. They come to look upon you as freemen; they have been your champions, and will be your friends in future difficulties. We simply ask you, in the name of your friends, in the name of the country, by your good conduct, by all that can elevate you and improve your condition, to show to your country, to even your old masters and mistresses, to everybody the world over, that it was a sin against God, a crime against you to hold you in slavery; to show that you were worthy to have your names enrolled among the freemen of the United States of America. (Great cheering.)

Judge KELLEY, member of Congress from Pennsylvania, was next introduced to the audience, and said:

MR. CHAIRMAN, AND MY FRIENDS—I am used to talking to pretty large audiences, and talking with a good deal of freedom, and I am not often confused at the beginning; but upon my word I do not know where to begin to-day, I have so much to say to you.

I have not come to you from Massachusetts. We had no William Lloyd Garrison to keep us up to our duty conscientiously. I come from Pennsylvania, a State—and by the way, I hope all Northern men here will note the fact, for it shows how bad it is to depart, however slightly, from a great principle—from Pennsylvania, which was the first to abolish slavery by legislative enactment in its own limits; and yet under the influences of corrupt politicians, forgot its first love of freedom, and gave as a great statesman, a President to the United States in James Buchanan, who, as President, betrayed the country in the name of slavery, and consented to the beginning of this war. (Groans.) A State, the first to abolish slavery, to make every man on its soil a citizen; which, in 1838, instead of sowing freedom, deprived every colored man within its limits of the right he had before enjoyed to citizenship and the exercise of suffrage. Bear her history in mind, oh! ye Northern men, and determine that, in beginning the work of reconstruction, we will make no departure from the requirements of absolute justice, and that we will decree that every man upon our soil shall enjoy all the rights of men; that we will measure for others by the standard we set up for ourselves, and not be content while any right we enjoy is withheld from another.

I will not, my colored friends, talk to you about the past. God knows that you understand it all too well. It is written in the depths of your hearts; it is with you in the morning and in the evening. When the dream disturbs your soul, it is by reason of the wrongs the white man has done you.

I turn to the hopeful future not to flatter, though I might very well entertain you with a favorable recital of your deeds during the last four years, but to remind you that, though it is true that you henceforth have no earthly master, you still have a master, the GREAT BEING, that strengthened and guided your eminent friend William Lloyd Garrison; (great cheering,) the Great Being that trained in humble poverty and simple-mindedness, Abraham Lincoln, a happy moulder of America's destiny; the good God whose stars shine together over the slave's hut as well as over your master's palaces. His laws you must obey. You must worship him not alone at the altar, but in every act of your daily life. It is not enough, it will not be enough that you are faithful in observing the Sabbath; that you go to Him with your sorrow; that you remember Him in your joys. You must remember that among His divine laws is that which reaches us all: "In the sweat of thy brow shalt thou eat thy bread." Labor, labor, is the law of all; and your friends in the North appeal to you to-day to stand by them, and help them in the great work they undertook to do for you: to do for the country as it is doing for you.

We want you to work with us, and we want you to do it by working here in South Carolina, and earning wages, taking care of your money, and making profit out of that money. Work on the plantation, if that is all you can do. Work in the workshop, if you can do it, and work well. He who does a day's work, and could have done it better, has cheated himself. Strive that your work on Monday shall be better done than it was on Saturday; and when Saturday comes round again, you shall be able to do a more skillful day's work.

We at the North learn three or four trades; and when one of you finds that you can do better for himself and his family by changing his pursuit, if he be assured of it, let him change it. We white boys at the North do not care much about being born to poverty. We don't care much of being deprived of education, in its broader sense, in early life. Why, it is only a stimulus. We run a race against a rich man's son carrying weight, and when we beat him under the weight we feel the prouder for it. Thus the truly great man who has addressed you toiled through the earlier years of his manhood, as well as his boyhood. Yet what South Carolinian of the last generation has had his name written higher in the scroll of fame, or graven more deeply in the hearts of the American people, than that of Henry Wilson, of Massachusetts. (Great cheering.)

The humble individual who now addresses you, never saw the light of day in a school-house after he was eleven years old ; and yet I know boys who went through college, whose cases I have tried as a judge, and whose interests I have represented in the Congress of my country. Now remember that we are all men, and what one man can do in Massachusetts, and another in Pennsylvania, you can do here ; and though the colored man is not allowed to vote in my State, I think I will write to my eloquent friend here, (Dickerson) to come and stump the district with me at the next election. I think he would show some of my constituents that we have no right to deprive the State of such intellectual power as he disclosed this morning. We have no right, my white brethren, to rob the commonwealth of such talent. (Cheers.)

I do like to look at these women here. I have a great respect for women; my mother was one, you know. (Laughter.) My wife is a woman. (Continued laughter.) But when I was not an abolitionist, while I was under the delusion that the old slave-masters used to teach, that you were little better than brutes, I never read or heard the story of a woman being outraged that my fingers did not tingle, and my blood swell from my heart to the throat. You are to be the mothers or wives of freemen's homes, and you must make those homes happy. You are to be the mothers of American citizens. You must strive to make them intelligent, educated, moral, patriotic and religious men. Many of you cannot read. You are not too old yet, and the mother that can read, can half educate her own child by helping it with its lessons ; and the mother that has little learning will get a great deal more by striving to hear the child's lessons, and so too, with the father. See to it that you make home happy, and then see to it that the good man makes home comfortable. You are not going to live in a slave hut. Work industriously ; work, be true, and then see that the carpet on your floor is one to your wife's taste. You can get at the conscience and heart of a great many Northern men who now think of you only—may I be pardoned for quoting the language in this sacred building—as "damned niggers;" you can get at their heart and conscience right straight through their pockets. And when they find that the colored farmer wants to buy goods from them, and that the colored tradesman has a great deal of money to spend, they will begin to think that you are Mr. John Jenkins and Mr. Joseph Brown. (Great laughter.) You are not to be contented with the common schools of Charleston for your children.

I am sorry that I do not know my colored friend's name, who spoke this morning. (Cries of Dickerson, Dickerson.) Well, if Dickerson had been well trained in his youth, and put in a good preparatory school, passed through that with honor and credit, and then entered the law office of John C. Calhoun, I have no doubt, nor can any one who heard him, doubt that he would have been one of the most distinguished lawyers of South Carolina to-day. (Tremendous cheers.) You may as well pay your fees in future to some lawyer Dickerson, as to a lawyer with a fairer face, and I have no doubt in the world, that colored physicians will attend your women with as perfect attention, as the kindest physician in the State. Just now you are to give your children the best education you can. Our Northern colleges are founded to make two things out of, reputation and money for the Professors; and when you are ready to send four or five hundred students to a University, you will find the University wlll be there to receive them. I am laying out a pretty big job for you. It is not a bit too big. Don't you know that colored men distinguished themselves in a harder job than that at Battery Wagner, at Olustee, and almost a hundred fields of battle? You can do in your quiet homes, and in your daily life, what they have done upon the field. Show your manhood and womanhood. I am only asking you to do what millions have done before; what you too might have done, had the opportunity offered.

I was just going to mention one of your number—one whose name has been sung and honored. One of your number is Captain Small, of the steamer "Planter." He took part in the celebration yesterday. I heard that he was here. If he is, I want to see and know him.

[The speaker then alluded to the invasion of a town in Pennsylvania, by Early's army: the name of the town we failed to catch.]

He said when Early's army approached the town, the Burgess walked out eight miles to surrender the town, and ask for its protection. That Burgess was David Small.

Robert Small, being entrusted with a steamer and steam engine, which it was never supposed he could ever get out, did run it out, and did, therefore, make the circle complete for yesterday's celebration. The white soldier was there, the white sailor was there, and the black soldier and the black sailor, but they were there under white command. There was nothing at all to show that the negro could do without a leader; but there came the "Planter," which Robert Small, the black man, had taken by his own command from the armed State of South Carolina, showing that your race have enterprise, energy, capacity, and may be trusted to go alone, at least on steamboats. (Cheers and laughter.)

But I am detaining you too long. My friends from the North, these are to be our fellow-citizens. (Cheers.) It is for us to say how soon, and to use all our influence at home. I thank the good God that he has so interwoven our welfare with our justice to them, that if we do not, under the scourgings we have received, do justice to them now and at once, his plans for scourging us further are already disclosed. There is such a thing as the Confederate debt. How much it amounts to, you don't know, and I can't tell you. We know that it amounts to thousands of millions of dollars. There is, in my judgment, under Providence, but one mode of preventing the early assumption of that debt by the United States Government, and that is to protect yourselves, and the loyal citizens all over the South. Let me give you an idea. We have not altered the spirit of the rebels; we have not converted them so that they renounce the right of a State to secede. They still hold the war to be unconstitutional. Now, if we confine suffrage to the white man alone, in the revolted States, every Senator and every Representative returned to Congress, will be believers in the doctrine of secession, and deniers of the constitutional right of coercing States to remain in the Union. Vallandigham, Fernando Wood, and the men who controlled the Chicago Convention, have borne contempt and contumely for what was as dear to them as the apple of their eye; aye, have been four years in maintaining these doctrines; and if you send from the South its old representatives of secessionists, and yet you get the Northern element combined with them, they will refuse to provide payment for the interest of the Federal debt, unless you embrace theirs also. And they will hold by the pocket or its equivalent, the throat of every honorable man, who refuses his bonds, and some Northern compromiser will propose, as it will be made a tax on the industry of their Northern friends, that both debts be assumed by the United States. How can you prevent it? Why, educate the colored man; and when the new constitution is made, see that the colored man's right goes with it.

Now, my friends, I have shown you what I want you to do. I tell you, in closing, to remember that in earning money and saving it, and gaining education, and disclosing your moral virtues, you are helping us to vindicate your rights, and embody your freedom in the institutions of our common country. (Long continued cheering.)

Three cheers were also given for Pennsylvania, the Keystone State. The congregation then sung the hymn, "Roll, Jordan, roll," and several others.

At the conclusion, Mr. Garrison said:

Well, my friends, this is worth coming from Boston to see and hear. I want to say a word or two more, before we separate, but I want to hear some others before I shall speak to you again. If they occupy all the time it will be very well. You will simply understand, that my heart is with you, and my benediction. But I want the next speaker to be one not from this side of the Atlantic, not an American by birth, but an Englishman; and better than that still, one who has a heart as wide as the whole world, one to whom the colored race is as much indebted, as to any man living. You have heard of the slaves in the West India Islands. There were eight hundred thousand of them. Their chains were broken long ago, and for many years they have been rejoicing in their freedom. They had many friends in England, powerful advocates and determined supporters, but their liberation under God, was owing as much—shall I do injustice to the living or dead—owing more to the noble man who sits on this platform, than to any other person in the world—George Thompson.

And let me tell you that when I was in England, then the chains were breaking in regard to the slaves of the West India Islands. Did our friend then say, My work is done. I said to him, "But we have yet four millions, to have their chains broken in the United States. If you should come, you will be buffeted, spit upon, and scorned." He thought himself it would reach to that, but he said at once, "I will give myself to their liberation, as well as I did to those in the West India Islands, in 1834." He came, came over to be buffeted, scorned and persecuted, and was hunted like a wild beast, because he pleaded your cause. In every town he was mobbed. Assassins dogged his footsteps on the right and on the left; and we, his friends, were compelled to force him out of the country, to save his life, though he never thought of leaving on any consideration. He is here to-day. We became acquainted in 1833, in London for the first time, and have been one in spirit and purpose ever since. If there is one on this globe whom I love and revere, it is George Thompson, the universal advocate of universal liberty and emancipation. (Great cheering.)

A message was received at this point of the proceedings, from the Citadel Square, stating that a large crowd had collected there, and were waiting for speakers. After a short consultation, Judge Kellogg, member of Congress; Joseph Hoxie, Rev. Dr. Leavitt and Major Delaney, left the Church, and proceeded to the Square to address the crowds there.

SPEECH OF HON. GEORGE THOMPSON,

Before the Freedmen of Charleston, (S. C.,) in Zion Church, April 15, 1865.

Hon. George Thompson, on being introduced, said:

This is a great day for me, as it is a great day for you. You are joyful, and I am joyful. Your cup runneth over, so does mine. I rejoice because I have remembered you in bonds. As it happened with you when in bonds, I rejoice with you to-day, being in freedom as I also am free.

This is a jubilee, a spectacle, on which God and the holy angels, and the spirits of the just made perfect, look with approval.

This is an assembly, that commands the sympathy of all the wise and good throughout the world. I can scarcely believe it true, that I stand upon a platform or pulpit in the city of Charleston, in the State of South Carolina, having before me the inspiring, magnificent spectacle of between three and four thousand persons, who but yesterday were things, to-day are men and women. (Cheers.) It is hard to believe, that I am at once in the cradle and the grave of treason, secession and slavery. (Cheers.) But yet I believe it is true; for since I came into your city, I have performed all the functions appertaining to a living, working man. I have walked, talked, ate and drank.

What shall I say to you now that I am here? To me it has

been given to see two great, pure, signal, glorious triumphs effected. To me it has been given the unspeakable privilege of being a co-laborer with Wilberforce and Clarkson, who led the way in the great struggle for British abolition—the abolition of the infernal slave trade, and its child—slavery.

To me, also, it has been given to see their triumph; to see them go up to heaven, presenting at the throne of heavenly grace, a million of broken manacles, and Africa redeemed from her English spoiler.

Now it is my privilege to be the co-worker and companion in joy of the Wilberforce of America—William Lloyd Garrison. For thirty years and more my heart has been with you; with you on the plantation, with you on the auction-block, with you in your unrequited toil, with you in your sufferings, separations, and scourgings; and now I am with you in your freedom. (Cheers.) You are no more slaves of these States, for God created all his children free. A little while ago, I could say of my own country, but not of this:

> "Slaves cannot breathe in England. If their lungs
> Inhale our air, that moment they are free."

Little did I think that on this 15th of April, 1865, I should be able to stand in the centre of the city of Charleston, South Carolina, and say slaves cannot breathe in America. They touch this country's soil, their shackles fall, and they stand redeemed, free forever. (Cheers.) The excellent member of Congress from Pennsylvania, has been talking to you of the future, of what its rights and its duties will be. And it is to me a matter of sincere gratification, that you have pleading your cause to-day, and pleading it no less earnestly elsewhere, and in the high places of your republic; men of that excellent representative State, Pennsylvania.

My counsel to you would be, co-operate with those excellent men. They want not only to make you personally free, your bodies as well as the fruit of them, but they wish that you should be clothed with the privileges and rights of citizenship.

Now, many objections will be urged to the granting of this

right, though it is your right according to the very principles upon which the nationality of this country rests. And though those scruples may be removed and prejudices conquered, that the hands of your friends may be strengthened, see that by your own conduct you justify all that your friends say in reference to your fitness and capacity, not only to exercise those rights, but that power which belongs to citizens of the United States. You are citizens. But yesterday you were not even regarded as men.

You were human beasts of burden; you were animated, two-legged hoeing machines; you were bought and sold like beasts of burden.

But you are transformed into men and women, equal to the President of the United States, for he is a man and no more, and each of you of the male sex is a man, and no less. Every principle upon which your government was founded, regards you as equally entitled, with Abraham Lincoln himself, to exercise the rights and privileges of citizenship. Now you have to be obedient to the laws. And the leading members of Congress are with you. The praying people of the North are with you. This you know. They sought you with their prayers, while you were yet slaves, while yet secluded. Since Generals Grant and Sherman, and Sheridan and Banks, have given them permission to traverse the coast and soil of this country, they have come down to you in the shape of teachers, who have been appointed to administer to your temporal and physical wants, and prove that the North is awake, and has put on the garments of repentance, trying to make restitution to you, in that they saw the anguish of your souls. God also is with you. He has been raising the storm that has shaken this land; he has directed the whirlwind. He has decreed that, ere yet these States are one, ere yet the Constitution is established in its former extent, the slave shall be free, and justice satisfied.

America tried the experiment in 1789, of establishing upon this continent a Government, founded upon a compromise of human rights. It founded a Government, on complexional differences. It built a temple to liberty, and called upon the world to admire, aye, upon all its tribes but one, to enter into it. It shut out one class, and that was your class. There was no place for the negro there. The ordinary term of a human life has gone by. Where is the Union now? Slavery has betrayed and dismembered it.

The old edifice will have at least to be raised upon a popular, more solid, and more enduring foundation. Now is the time. Let the fundamental law upon which this republic shall rise, be the immutable law of right. If not, as the first temple has fallen, so shall the second. Sound policy, as well as duty, dictates to the people of this country, that they should base their Union upon a righteous principle.

What is it we who come from Europe, ask the people of America to do? What was my cry when I came here more than thirty years ago? Did I come seeking money of the Government? No! My message to the people of this country, was simply to loose the bands of wickedness, and let the oppressed go free. That was my message. Say unto my people, break every yoke. I said it was for the interest of all to do right.

I have, for the last fourteen months, and more, been traveling over the North. But what a revolution has taken place there! Thirty years ago, America vomited me out of her mouth. She spewed me forth, and drove me from her shores as a disturber, a fire-brand, an incendiary.

During the thirty years that have elapsed between my first and last visit, a revolution has taken place at the North. I left the colleges on the side of slavery. I returned and found the coleges on the side of liberty. I left America, when there was but one man in the house of Congress, who dared to present an anti-slavery petition. I returned, and found scarce a man in Congress, who would not deem himself honored by being selected to present such a petition. I left America, with the newspapers of the country, and the literature of the country on the side of slavery. I returned, and found the newspapers and literature, the best and most popular works published in the country, on the side of freedom. I find the man who towers the highest in the estimation of the people of the North, is the man most earnestly, most sincerely, most uncompromisingly devoted to the cause of freedom, of universal—impartial freedom.

I left America with the government itself on the side of slavery, —a slaveholder in the chair, and slaveholders ruling by them in the Senate and House of Representatives. Slaveholders had a great representation. Slaveholders governed East and West, North and South. They were not only lords on their own plantations, not only rulers of these sunny estates of the South, but absolute tyrants over the whole country. And I was sensible, in fine more sensible of slavery at Washington, than I am now sensible of the existence of slavery at the South.

Instead of Andrew Jackson of Tennessee, a slaveholder, in the chair, I find, when the men appointed had to select a Chief Magistrate, they passed over the heads of all the slaveholders ot this continent. They did not even select one of the greatest in eloquence, the best versed in political chicanery, but they selected one of humble origin, born, it is true, in a slave State, but a self-made man in a free State, a rail-splitter, a patriot soldier, honest Abraham Lincoln.

All the dominant, overruling elements are enlisted on your side. The great majority of the North have declared solemnly, in National Convention assembled, that slavery has been the cause of this late rebellion. They say it is adverse to republican institutions, and therefore must be utterly and forever abolished on this soil. All the elements to-day are in your favor. Spread your sails, and catch the auspicious breeze! Your President is with you in sympathy, in purpose, in the exercise of those large powers with which he is entrusted. He has spoken the word, and will not be content until that word is incarnated with the freedom of every slave in the United States.

In our notice of this meeting, we cannot do better than give place to the following paragraph, from the pen of Rev. A. P. Putnam:

"The enthusiasm of that assembled multitude, at the first mention, by one of the speakers, of the name of Abraham Lincoln, was such as to defy description. It was intense, wild and almost fearful. The vast crowd cheered and waved their handkerchiefs, some screaming for joy, and others raising their hands and clasping them in gratitude to God, and hundreds weeping the tears they could not repress, as they thought of their great friend and benefactor. How little did any of us dream that on that very morning, he lay silent in death at Washington. Who can tell what anguish of soul, the dread tidings will carry to the millions of God's poor at the South who have learned to love him, as their great and good deliverer. Heaven comfort their hearts, and grant that the President's successor may also prove their father and friend.

"Too much cannot be said in praise of Gen. Saxton, who is in command of that department. Faithful, vigilant, loyal and true to freedom, he commands the confidence of the Government, at Washington, and the admiration aud sympathy of every patriot, white or black, within the limits of his jurisdiction."

As it was not the good fortune of the writer to be present at this inside meeting, he gives the above able reports of the speeches, by the reporter of the "Charleston Courier," and the account of the subsequent exercises, as written by Mr. A. M. Powell, the correspondent of the N. Y. Tribune.

He says: "Judge Kelly spoke to them, as he has in

Congress, and elsewhere spoken for them; of the responsibility of citizens, which they are to assume, or should assume in the new government, to be established in the South. This point too, was well made by each of the other speakers. He spoke of the need and value of industry, to improve their homes, and to secure education and its advantages, for themselves and their children.

"The addresses of Messrs. Thompson and Tilton were exceedingly well adapted to the occasion, and fully worthy of those gentlemen. It was a great meeting, and will mark distinctly the beginning of a new era. Mr. Redpath told them of Wendell Phillips, whom they much wanted to see and hear, and they voted to invite Mr. Phillips, to address them in Charleston, on the 4th of July next. They voted with an emphasis so loud and strong, that Mr. Phillips might well nigh have heard it in Boston. Their invitation was extended also to the American Anti-Slavery Society, and to Frederick Douglass, to meet with them on the next national anniversary."

AN OUTSIDE MEETING.

"Outside of the Church, while the meeting, of which I have spoken was in progress, the Rev. Theodore L. Cuyler, of Brooklyn, addressed a very interesting gathering, of about 2000 children. They commissioned him to write to Mr. Lincoln, and invite him to visit them in Charleston. Young and old, seemed everywhere to regard Mr. Lincoln as a father and friend; whom their masters hated so much, they seem to feel that they can trust. Another meeting, at the same time, immense in numbers, upon Citadel Square, was addressed by Judge Hoxie, of New York, a Senator from Michigan, Major Delaney, and others. At the close of the meeting, a large procession was formed, with bands of music, and paraded the streets. It was a great occasion for Charleston."

It was with reference to this procession, without doubt, that Mr. Cuyler wrote to the "Evangelist."

"On Saturday morning last, I was standing in front of St. Michael's Church, with Wm. Lloyd Garrison. Just then the band of the 127th Regiment came down Meeting Street, playing *Old John Brown*, most superbly.

"'Only listen to that in Charleston streets!' exclaimed Garrison, and we both broke into tears. I had many such startling and almost incredible surprises, during my visit. For example I stood with Ward Beecher, Garrison, George Thompson, the English Reformer, and Theodore Tilton, beside the grave of John C. Calhoun, in St. Phillip's Churchyard. It is a plain brick oblong tomb, covered with a marble slab, and bearing the single word 'CALHOUN.' 'There,' said Garrison, lies a man whose name is decayed worse than his mouldering form; the one may have a resurrection, the other never!' Several northern shells, have fallen and burst near that tomb! Did none of the bones in that sepulchre *rattle*, when the voice of William Lloyd Garrison, was heard at the grave's mouth?"

Leaving now the records of these wonderful "Freedmen's Meetings," with the regret that we have not all the addresses upon that memorable occasion, reported in full, we return to explorations and incidents in other parts of the city.

We may first notice however, that the "Citadel" itself, together with the famous Orphan Asylum, is now used as a barrack for colored troops, who flock into our army at the rate of about one hundred per day.

The splendid marble Custom House, which was in process of erection at the outbreak of the war, though standing on the margin of the harbor, escaped the iron missiles with but little damage. It is now being stored with the confiscated cotton which is rapidly arriving.

The long Market extending from Meeting street to the harbor gives evidence, at the upper end, of the revival of business. The stalls are rented by negroes and Germans for $1 per week, where they carry on the meat business in a small way, and making a bare livelihood. Very little money is in circulation yet. Confederate notes were bought by the bushel at a nominal price, and carried away as curiosities by our steamer's company.

We found the price-list lower than in New York, though it must be confessed that the quality of the meat was also decidedly lower.

Sirloin steak sold for 25 cents a pound; Mutton from

20 to 25 cents; Veal, 25 cents; Butter, 65 cents; Lard, 30 cents; Cheese, 25 cents.

"In Federal money, we presume," we said.

"Certainly," replied the ebony salesman.

"But how much in Confederate currency?"

"Oh, sar, we better *gib* it to you, sar!"

Potatoes and green peas were abundant, and we were told that strawberries would be in market in a few days. Behind some of the stalls were well-dressed and handsome mulatto girls, having bouquets of choice flowers for sale. Advancing toward the river, the market became more and more deserted, and the stalls entirely empty.

St. Michael's Church, with its tall tower, which had been a target for the Federal gunners, was viewed with much interest. A large shell hole adorns the middle of the tower, while another through the rear wall, let daylight into the darkened sanctuary, demolished the altar, and, according to Mr. Cuyler, "*broke* the commandments, graven on tables of stone, the discriminating missile sparing the three commandments, "Thou shalt not steal—thou shalt not kill—thou shalt not commit adultery—the very precepts that Charleston needed most." We trust *that* shell will receive full absolution, since that was its first and last offense against the commandments. Seven of the bells belonging to the chime of this Church were melted into cannon on account of the scarcity of metal.

Another Church, whose name we do not recollect,

had been very rudely handled, being but little better than a crumbling ruin.

The little "Church of the Huguenots," in semi-Gothic style, attracted the observation of all. It is built of greyish stone, and stands in the midst of a rural kirk-yard, which must once have possessed great beauty. There the tall trees still wave over mossy and mouldering graves, ploughed by cannon shot, and slabs broken by the exploding shell. In their branches were singing the mocking birds as in other days, and in their dense shadow still bloomed the wild-brier rose and trailing jassmine. A cow was browsing from the mounds of the graves, and as we stood musing upon the devastation of war, and the awful retribution which has come upon the devoted city, two carrion crows, with hoarse and dissonant cawing, rose out of the boughs above our heads; and, flapping their great white-tipped wings, flew lazily across the street and perched upon a lofty dwelling. Alas! thought we, the crows and buzzards sitting on ruined towers and spires, dressed in deepest black, are almost the only mourners over the scathed and blasted city!

The interior of the Church is sadly ruined. Two immense holes upon either side, just beneath the cornice, show where the destroyers entered. The chandeliers were struck and shivered, whole tiers of pews were torn up, and the walls frightfully scarred. Piles of stones and wood and rubbish lie about the floors. Prayer books and hymn books, cushions, dirt and dust complete the scene of confusion. Happily, the marble tablets, with their inscriptions in French and English, have been spared. However just one might feel all this punishment to be, it would be impossible to exult over such a spectacle.

Nearly opposite the "Church of the Huguenots," is the old "Planter's Hotel," long since rendered uninhabitable. It was fairly riddled. Since the occupation of the city by our forces, permission has been given to Mrs. Eliza Havens to live in its rooms, and teach her little school.

This woman was born at the North, has lived in Charleston twenty years, and throughout the entire war, was a declared and unflinching Unionist. She has suffered incredible hardships, having been twice shelled from her house by day, and once at night; threatened with imprisonment and death, robbed of all property—some $12,000 at the beginning of the war—and reduced to actual beggary. We found her standing at the door of the Hotel, very meanly dressed, and bearing every mark of suffering upon her countenance. She gave us the most cordial welcome. She declares that the old flag has always been "her soul's delight," and that she often sang "The Star Spangled Banner" in the streets of Charleston, with her enemies on every side. How trustworthy these statements may be, we leave others to judge. Upon stating the case to the passengers in the evening, a purse of $25 was raised for her; which, added to contributions by the kindly

Mr. Edward Ball and others, made the sum of $35—sufficient for present exigencies. Her case was referred for further investigation to our worthy Mayor, who was to remain in the city a few days longer.

The "Charleston Hotel" was the only one open at that time, and was kept by Mr. J. P. Stetson, brother of the present proprietor of the Astor House, New York. It was crowded during our sojourn to overflowing, and its tables were said to be inviting.

The "Mills House" was utterly tenantless.

The "Circular Church," or all that remains of it, was interesting only from the fact, that within it, the first secession sermon was preached. Nothing but portions of its walls, and half of the tower remain. Within, the enclosure is overgrown with grass and weeds, upon which cattle would find good browsing.

Next to it is the ruin of "Institute Hall," of which scarcely one stone or brick is left upon another. Here the "Ordinance of Secession" was passed by five hundred majority. Here also the Convention was held which nominated Stephen A. Douglass for the Presidency. Passing down Hayne street, we came to the "Ration House," or, as it is called by the proprietor, "The Invalid's Commissary."

Standing, sitting and lying around the entrances, were hundreds of poor freedmen and women, in every stage of raggedness,—waiting their turn to be served. Elbowing our way through this heterogeneous crowd, we entered the immense stores of Mr. George W. Williams.

Circular Church.

Ruins of Institute Hall.

CHARLESTON IN RUINS.

We found this gentleman superintending his work. He is of medium size, long, sandy, curling hair, and benign countenance, and received us with great cordiality. His stores, divided by a central partition, with a large space for inter-communication, contain in the right apartment, hundreds of bags of rice, corn, meal and grits, and in the other, the large bins in which these are emptied for distribution. The needy recipients enter, one at a time, receive a ticket at the counter, and on presenting it, with their little bags, are served with a peck, or half a peck, of rice or grist. We stood and watched these beggared people. It was a pitiful sight—children, old men and women, of every shade, came eagerly up and held out their bags for the ration. One girl, of excessive blackness, and more completely tatterdemalion, than any we had seen, presented her ticket for one half peck of rice. The negro filled her bag, and she went out. Immediately following her, was a woman of thirty-five years, perfectly white, of haggard countenance, and dressed in rusty black. She advanced, held out her ticket for a peck of rice, and received it. As she turned, she said:

"Can't you give me a little *salt* to-day?"

"We haven't any salt left," replied the waiter.

With a sigh, she left the store. Turning towards Mr. Williams, in our surprise, we asked.

"What is *that white* woman doing here?"

"My dear sir," replied Mr. W., "that woman, four

years ago, was worth half a million dollars, and lived in a fine mansion on the Battery."

He then stated the fact before mentioned, that the cashier of the Bank of Charleston, comes every day to his store, to get his peck of rice or meal.

At our request, Mr. Williams wrote out a brief statement, concerning his work, which he brought to the "Oceanus," just before we sailed. It cannot fail to interest all our readers, and we therefore transcribe it in full.

STATEMENT OF MR. GEO. S. WILLIAMS.

"Since the occupation of Charleston, by the U. S. troops, about three million pounds of provisions, consisting of rice, grist, meal and salt, have been issued to the poor and needy citizens of Charleston, of all classes, colors and conditions. Many who were considered millionaires, a few years since, are reduced by the war, to want, penury and beggary, and are to be seen carrying their bags of rations through the streets of Charleston.

"The Confederate Government, in one way and another, absorbed all the capital of the banks, and various monied institutions, of the city and state. The failure of Jeff. Davis & Co., necessarily breaks the monied institutions, on which the people relied for support. The large amount of provisions being issued, was accumulated by the city and Confederate authorities.

"Geo. W. Williams, one of the aldermen of the city, and chairman of the Subsistence Committee, has devoted his whole time for the past two years to distributing this food to the poor.

"The Confederate authorities, turned over to him all the stores owned by them, to be distributed under direction of the City Council, to the poor of Charleston.

"A large amount of these supplies, was destroyed in the burning of the cotton, and the explosion at the North East Railroad Depot. On the landing of the Union forces, Mr. Williams furnished Col. Bennet, with a list of the stores, and secured a guard to protect them. These supplies were taken possession of by the U. S. Government, and turned over to a committee of three, to be distributed to the poor of Charleston and vicinity.

"The large storehouses of Geo. W. Williams & Co., on Hayne Street, are used as a depot for distributing rations. Tickets are issued to needy families, two-thirds being colored; and thousands of the recipients are to be seen daily wending their way to the 'Invalid's Commissary,' for food.

"These supplies will soon be exhausted, and then What will become of this helpless and suffering people? A number of tickets have been issued to colored people, who have reached their *four score and twenty*, (five score or 100?) This class of citizens, are supplied at their own homes."

The importance of the question asked by Mr. Williams, can hardly be over-estimated. These poor dependent people cannot be left to starvation, and at present there is little which can employ their hands in the way of industry. We spent much time in sounding their disposition, now that they are free. Not one expressed an expectation, or desire that they should be fed long at the Government expense. All promptly said, "We want to work and get our own living; we want something to do, and we will work all the harder for being free."

It would be false to deny that these people are ignorant. How *could* they be anything else? They need instruction in the very rudiments of education, and self-supporting industry, economy and thrift. But never were a people more willing, and eager to be taught. They are *naturally* intelligent and shrewd. Steady and wholesome instruction, will make them useful and efficient, as they always have been law-abiding citizens. He who should expect them to step at once into the full daylight of freedom, from the long, dark night of bondage, without being somewhat dazzled, and needing some safe guide to lead them, would justly win a reputation for folly, not far removed from insanity. The work of their melioration and elevation, will be slow, but it will be sure, for the material upon which to work is there—willing hearts, strong hands, and gratitude to their benefactors.

MAGNOLIA CEMETERY.

Taking a horse and wagon, both of which had come down from a former generation, and for which the avaricious proprietor *asked* the modest sum of $5, we rode through the pleasant fields, two miles out of the city, to Magnolia Cemetery, the principal burying ground of Charleston. The road was flanked by high hedges, overgrown with wild briar roses of unusual size, and trees adorned with long grey beards of moss. The cemetery has once enjoyed high culture, and a reputation for great beauty. Natural water-courses, or tide-ways, wind at will through its whole expanse, and the hand of the horticulturist has done much to increase its charms. Not many splendid monuments are there; the prevailing remembrances of the dead being the plain slab, erect, or laid flat above the graves. A garden well kept, and abounding in flowers, adorns the centre. One monument alone gives celebrity to this burial-place. It is a pile of marble, of variegated colors, elaborately carved and wrought into mosaic figures, of remarkable beauty. It is the tribute of a husband to his wife, and for four years his own hands have been employed upon the labor of love.

An old negro, of intense blackness, was our guide through this city of the dead. He pointed out the graves of some distinguished South Carolinians, but the natural beauty of the place eclipses all that art has done to enhance its attractiveness. He told us that four years ago, he stood at the outer limit of the cemetery, and watched the bombardment of Sumter; the whole panorama being distinctly visible. The keeper of the garden permitted us to pick from its exuberance of flowers, the most exquisite boquets of roses. Scores of our party visited this cemetery.

THE N. E. RAILROAD DEPOT.

This tragic spot was viewed with the most painful interest. The accounts of the explosion vary somewhat, as to the premeditated slaughter which was effected there. By a few, it is claimed that no intention of massacre can be charged upon the principals in the deed. But in the light of all these recent developments, the cold-blooded and atrocious conspiracies; the deliberate starving of our prisoners; the fiendish introduction of yellow-fever into Newbern, and the attempt to do the same in New York; the St. Alban's raid; and the attempt to burn New York,—the most probable account is that which is the most generally believed, to wit: that when the Rebels were forced to evacuate the city, they resolved to blow up this dépôt, where the Confederate supplies were stored. The poor people were told to go there and help themselves. Soon a crowd, consisting mostly of slaves, was gathered there. Major Pringle had mined the premises, and was not to be kept from, nor delayed in his purpose, although so many lives would be destroyed. By some it is averred that two or three warnings of this intention were given. Grant that there were, does this palliate the deed? Who but a fiend incarnate, would have given the order to apply the match, until he *knew* that all the innocent and helpless were safe from harm? The train was fired, and in an instant three hundred—according to some authorities four hundred—human beings were blown into eternity. Not long after this occurrence, this Pringle was captured by colored troops, belonging to our army, which insufferable indignity to his royal Carolinian blood, so frenzied him, as to betray him into the best act of his life, as concerning mankind, the blowing out of his own brains with a pistol.

THE RACE COURSE.

Rev. J. L. Corning, the correspondent of the "N. Y. Sun," thus speaks of this locality, which it was not the writer's mournful pleasure to visit:

"The old race-course, about a mile outside of the city, was the great "prison-pen," where thousands of Union soldiers suffered horrors which Heaven only can record. On this accursed, yet thrice hallowed spot, during a long and stormy winter, our brave captured boys lay hungry and shelterless. I do not mean to exaggerate—I mean literally *shelterless.* The ground for the space of five square acres is to-day covered with holes, into which the poor victims crawled like beasts of the forest, to hide themselves from the driving storms. Patches of earth, from six to eight feet square, are marked off, all over the dreary plain, by ditches dug around them, and upon these they lay through rainy days and nights, as the best protection that could be invented against the pouring floods. A plain board fence, on one side of this acaldema, encloses the burial-ground; and here, as they died, they were shoveled into the earth like dogs. Over two-hundred head-boards can be counted in the yard; but these only avail to keep up a semblance of decent respect for the name and memory of the departed. Identification is impossible, and the weeping kindred will only recognize the faces that are gone, when they become radiant in the better land, in the last glorious gathering of the good and brave."

And lest these words of the "Sun correspondent," might be thought extravagant, let us see how another observer was impressed by the same spectacle of suggestive horrors. Rev. A. P. Putnam thus writes to the "Independent." After noticing the war-scathed and utterly desolate situation of the city, he writes:

"Whatever feeling of pity one may entertain for those who suffer woes like these, is likely to be dissipated, to a great extent, by a visit to the race-course, just outside of the city, where thousands of our prisoners were confined by the rebel authorities. Here is a field of ten acres, without a tree or roof to afford the least shelter from the burning heat of the sun, or the pitiless blasts of the storm. Here, at times, as many as 10,000 of our soldiers were kept under guard, night and day, summer and winter, with no canopy above them, but the arching sky, and no bed for repose, but the cold, damp earth. The whole surface of their prison-grounds is intersected with little trenches, which our brave boys dug with their hands, in order better to keep dry, in wet weather, the places where they were obliged to lie. Here and there also, they had scooped out large excavations, into which they might crawl and keep warm, when the winds were chill and the storm severe. All over this field, many a noble fellow suffered in his wounds, and from disease and starvation. Some of them, as they died, were denied sepulture by the rebels, and were buried on the spot, by their comrades, who dug their graves as best they could. Others, three hundred in number, were borne a little distance to a rising ground, and were laid side by side in the earth, in several parallel rows, with no stone or mark to tell their names to the visitor. Hither, to the race-course, the fashionable people of the city, were wont to take their afternoon drives; and, at a little distance from our men, would sit smoking their cigars and drinking their juleps, while surveying through their eye-glasses, with the utmost complacency, if not with the keenest delight, the horrible sufferings of the defenders of the Union. It was nightfall when I was there. The proud Carolinian, the cruel guard, the multitude of heroes,—all were gone.

Yet there were the innumerable trenches and excavations, which the hands of our braves had made,—there the cold bed of earth, where they had lain, and where so many of them had sickened and died at last—and there, at a little distance, were the unknown graves of the martyrs, to the sacred cause of Union and Liberty. The wind sighed mournfully through the pine trees, that surrounded the little cemetery, which our own troops had recently enclosed by a neat fence, and I came away, feeling that it was one of the saddest scenes I had ever witnessed; and feeling too, how just had been the judgments of God, which had rained down destruction upon that rebellious and cruel city."

Upon returning to the "Oceanus," at 5 o'clock P. M., we learned that the pilot had declared his unwillingness to take the steamer over the bar by twilight, and the time of our departure had been again postponed until the next high tide, at 8 o'clock Sunday morning. The majority of the party, very weary by the day's explorations, were glad to spend the evening quietly on board. A few, however, paid a visit to the house of Col. Beecher, to witness a very unique and impressive presentation to his brother, Henry Ward Beecher. One of the witnesses, the Editor of the "The Union," gives the subjoined account.

"It was made by a band of ten colored women of Charleston, who had, at an early period, formed an association for the purpose of aiding our sick and wounded prisoners, in the hands of the Rebels.

"The difficulties which they had overcome were very great, and the fidelity and courage they had shown, such as every honest man must pay a tribute of respect to. Three of them had been publicly whipped with seventy lashes, for the work they were engaged in, and all of them, compelled to work all day for their own support, had courted this outrage by devoting half of the night to their holy labor. I did not arrive in time to hear their remarks; those of Mr. Beecher in reply, were simple and touching. He promised them the appreciation of the North, and told them that there was a movement there to place the black equal before the laws, with the white, so that they might, free from hindrance, become what they could and would. No scene in Charleston touched me more than this."

The evening on board was spent in general conversation, comparison of relics, and musical entertainment, and at an earlier hour than usual, the cabins were deserted and silent.

CHAPTER VII.

The morning of Sabbath, April 16th, dawned without a cloud. The air was balmy and incense-laden. The dews of the night had allayed the feverish sultriness of the day before. It was a matter of some regret to many that our departure should have been delayed until Sunday, but we were in the hands of the pilot, whose decision to that effect was final. We must go when he was ready to take us safely over the bar. Three or four of our passengers were to remain for a few days in the city, among whom were Mayor Wood, of Brooklyn, and Rev. J. L. Corning, whom we regretted to leave behind. The crowd assembled upon the wharves to witness our departure. About 9 o'clock we bade adieu to our friends on shore, many of whom were the gentlemanly officers whose attentions had made our stay in the city so delightful; glanced once more at the shot-scarred houses along the Battery, and the curious crowd that lined the docks, and while the band sweetly played the farewell and yet inviting melody, "Home, Sweet Home!" we moved slowly out into the waters of the harbor. Again, we waved salutations to the monitors and vessels of war; again were we abreast of Fort Sumter, which in that Sabbath sunlight seemed more than ever consecrated to Freedom. We could not pass it by, perhaps, never to look upon its storied walls again, without the voice of sacred song. We uncovered our heads as we stood upon the hurricane and quarter decks. What should meet the demand of our emotion save the Old Doxology again! With tearful eyes and tremulous voices, we sang once more "Praise God from whom all blessings flow!" The sentinels within the fort gave answer to the strain by dipping the colors and waving their bayonets, which flashed in the sun. Then again we sang the appropriate and touching words—

"Out on an ocean all boundless we ride,
We're homeward bound, homeward bound!
Toss'd on the waves of the rough, restless tide,
We're homeward bound, homeward bound!"

Who shall smile at the mention of tears of joy? Strong, brave-hearted, noble men shed them then and there! Reluctantly we turned away from the grand old ruin now sinking in the distance. Our eyes had seen the "glory of the nation" ascend to supremacy above its crumbled walls. Our ears had heard the music of its waving folds; our hearts had drunk deeply of the inspiration of that hour. That was a day to be marked "with a white stone" in the calendar of every son and daughter of Columbia. Other scenes might be effaced from memory's tablet, but *that, never.* And as we "thought thereon, we wept," tears of patriotic pride and exultation, yet attempered by the remembrance of the *price* at which the triumph had been purchased.

At length the bar was crossed; the pilot dismissed, and we were alone again upon the broad-breasted, blue and briny ocean.

Nothing could exceed the loveliness of those Sabbath skies, full of light and peace from horizon to horizon, and the bosom of the sea, breathing always with heave and swell, and then unbroken by a single white cap or the leap from its surface of a single one of its finny dwellers,

> "Sweet day, so cool, so calm, so bright,
> Bridal of earth and sky,"

How appropriate that we should unite in worship and praise of Him "whose way is in the sea," and "whose path is upon the great waters."

At 11 o'clock, religious services were held in the Ladies Cabin, conducted by Rev. Mr. Cuyler.

It was Easter Sabbath, and the opening hymn was an appropriate recognition of the great fact of the Saviour's Resurrection.

The Rev. Mr. Putnam read the Scripture, and offered, the Introductory Prayer.

Rev. Mr. Cuyler then preached a timely, impressive, and eloquent sermon from Philipians 3, 13:

"Brethren, I count not myself to have apprehended, *but this one thing I do!*"

The Closing Prayer was offered by Rev. J. C. French.

In the afternoon at 5 o'clock, services were again held, conducted by Rev. H. M. Gallaher, who took for his text, Numbers 32, 23:—"*And be sure your sin will find you out!*" His sermon was illustrative, pungent, and practical.

The Closing Prayer was offered by Rev. Mr. Chadwick.

In the evening a meeting for general conference and prayer was held, in which a number of laymen as well as clergymen took part. The entire day was fittingly and profitably occupied. There were none on board who appeared to forget that it was the *Sabbath.* All merriment was hushed; becoming seriousness ruled every hour. The influence of that "Lord's day" will not be lost.

Monday passed without any incident worthy of special remark. The sky was cloudless, and though a smart breeze from the North lashed the sea into white-capped billows; and, as we rounded Cape Hatteras, sometimes dashed the spray upon the quarter deck, yet the steamer, cutting the waves at right angles, had far less motion than upon the downward trip, and very few on board were sea-sick.

In the evening, a meeting was called, at which it was resolved to have no speeches; but, after transacting miscellaneous business, to devote the time to musical exercises. Mr. Wm. B. Bradbury was appointed to conduct them. The Plymouth Collection was used. All joined in singing many of its best and most familiar tunes, in some of which, the singers were accompanied by the brass band, producing a grand and solemn effect.

At the close of the meeting, seven of the colored waiters came into the cabin, and for an hour delighted the company with their chorusses, accompanied by two guitars. The sweetness, compass, and power of some of their voices surprised us. They sang only the choicest of modern ballads and quartettes. The look of intense disgust which mantled the features of Helon Johnson, their leader, when asked to sing "Carry me back to Old Virginny," and his disdainful reply, "We don't sing that *negro trash*," were something to be remembered.

Tuesday morning arose with the beauty of the day preceding. The passengers were upon the decks, elate with the recollections of the past few days, buoyant with delight as they saw at the left, the distant line of the shore, and at the right, the deep green of the sea dissolving into a deeper blue, and with the prospect of soon being at anchor in the waters of Hampton Roads. When about thirty miles from Fortress Monroe, our attention was called to a large steamer far out in the offing, with her flag at half-mast. It was a matter of temporary wonder for whom this signal of mourning could be displayed. We now saw a pilot-boat bearing towards us, her colors also at half-mast. When within hailing distance, a passenger shouted:

"What's the news?"

The reply came back faintly, but with startling accents, over the water.

"The President is dead!" and the pilot boat passed on.

Every face on board the "Oceanus" turned pale. For a moment every tongue was mute. At last, we said among ourselves: "It cannot be!" "It is a cruel hoax which these men have perpetrated to cloud our joy." "We do not believe it." And so half hoping, yet cruelly tantalized, we obeyed the summons to the breakfast table. But it was little indeed that we refreshed ourselves in that gloomy cabin. Coming again on deck, we discovered another pilot-boat approaching, with the ominous signal of sorrow drooping midway from the yard-arm.

Again the earnest shout:

"What's the news?"

Again the reply—"*President Lincoln is dead!*"

"*How did he die?*"

"HE WAS ASSASSINATED!"

The blood curdled at every heart. "Assassinated! When! How! Where! By whom! For what!" Oh, what a torture of suspense! What a horrible termination to all our exultancy! Why were the doors of our souls thus rudely torn open, and such a great agony rolled in upon them! We walked in silence up and down the decks. We went to our staterooms, and poured out the irrepressible tears. We looked in each others faces for some gleam of hope or comfort. We brooked impatiently the slow progress of the steamer. We imagined woes and anarchies throughout the land. We breathed at times the patriot's curse upon the hearts that conceived, and the hands that executed, the deed of Hell.

We prayed God to make an utter and awful end of the system, which alone could breed such monster-demons upon the earth. Our steamer was a seething cauldron of grief and indignation.

At last we touched the dock at Fortress Monroe, and received the New York papers, with full particulars of the crime and the martyrdom; the attempt upon Mr. Seward's life, and the contemplated taking off of Gen. Grant, and the entire Cabinet.

We were invited to visit the Fortress. At any other time that immense and splendid work, with its grey walls and deep moat, its monster guns, its casemates, its magazines, its green fields and opening foliage, its commanding prospect of the "Roads," and the large fleet of Government vessels, of the "Rip Raps," and the historic locality where the "Monitor" and "Merrimac," decided national and naval problems for all coming time,—at any other time, these would have commanded our absorbed attention, and awakened our enthusiasm.

But now we walked mechanically towards the entrance, gazed mournfully upon the drapery of black, with which the Provost-Marshal's and Quartermaster's offices were shrouded; the dear face of the departed

President above their entrances, and framed in crape; we were "like them that dream," as we moved in slow procession along the parapets, scarcely noticing the wonderful armament of the Fortress, and the panorama on every hand, and in less than an hour, returned to the steamer, weary, heart-sick and desolate.

Not the least touching and impressive spectacle, was the grief of the colored men, women and children, who sat by the wayside or moved about as if bewildered and deserted.

One woman of middle age, whom we met as we came out of the Fortress, had not heard of Mr. Lincoln's death. When informed of it, she threw up her arms with a wild cry of despair, wrung her hands, sank down upon the grass, and bursting into a flood of tears, exclaimed, "O Lord! O Lord! what *shall* we do now? what *shall* we do now?" There were few dry eyes among those who witnessed that sight.

A number of these black people, were sitting around a table, upon which they had eggs and a few articles of provision for sale.

Upon being asked what they thought of Mr. Lincoln's death, one replied: "We must jes pray all de more!" Another said: "Our father is gone! But dey can't kill de Lord, I'se sure of dat?" And still another in similar strain:

"Oh! we hab lost our dear father; but bress the Lord, dere is one friend we hab above dat they can't shoot—de Lord Almighty, He's above us all."

And so we knew the cry of wailing and anguish, would go up from every rice and cotton field of all the South, from these trusting creatures, and from every dusky mourner between both oceans, from whose hands the beloved martyr had smitten the accursed chains, and that cry would enter the ear of the Lord of Hosts, who has written, "Vengeance is mine, I will repay."

The brief visit at Fortress Monroe, made scarcely a definable impression, save that of universal gloom. It had been proposed to make flying calls at Norfolk, Portsmouth; and, if a permit could be obtained from the Secretary of War, to spend a day at Richmond, but the spirit of sight-seeing was crushed. We felt that responsible duties called us home, and decent respect for the dead at the Capital, required us to appear no longer in the capacity of excursionists. Returning on board the "Oceanus," a meeting was called to decide upon our course. A vote being taken, it was resolved, by a large majority, to proceed directly, and with all despatch, to New York. After taking on a supply of water, the steamer was again under way homeward.

A considerable number of our party left us at Fortress Monroe, to go to Washington, and attend the funeral of the President, upon the following day. Among these, we noticed Messrs. Cyrus P. Smith, Bryan H. Smith, Charlton T. Lewis, S. L. Husted and daughter, E. J. Ovington and lady, together with others, whose absence we regretted.

Just before leaving the wharf, a fireman, in shoveling coal in one of the bunkers, discovered three blockade-runners, who had escaped from confinement in Charleston, and stolen their passage northward in our steamer. They were handed over to the authorities, and placed in the lock-up of Fortress Monroe. Two other vagabonds, who had stowed themselves away below, after we landed at the Fortress, were also brought to light, and led off from the steamer, with wrath and vengeance upon their ugly faces. It was a relief to be rid of these not doubtful characters.

Providence smiled upon us out of the heavens, with the most propitious weather on our homeward way.

The last *evening* meeting, was called at 8 o'clock P. M.; which, at the suggestion of Rev. T. L. Cuyler, and with the approval of all on board, resolved itself into a permanent Association, or "Club," to be known as the "*Sumter Club*." A committee was appointed to draw up a suitable Constitution, and name officers for the ensuing year.

A committee was also appointed to prepare and publish a memorial volume of the trip and its incidents, and another committee to provide an appropriate badge, to designate membership of the "Club." Brief addresses were made, and hymns sung, in harmony with the theme which was upon every heart, and the meeting adjourned to half-past 10 o'clock Wednesday morning.

We again allude to the smooth seas and the matchlessly beautiful weather of this final day of the trip. Save the unbreaking undulation, from which the sea is never free, its surface was as glassy and calm as that of an inland lake.

At half-past 10 o'clock, according to adjournment, we assembled for the final business meeting.

The committee appointed to organize the "Sumter Club," reported, through its chairman, Rev. Mr. Cuyler, as follows:

"The passengers of the steamer "Oceanus," returning from its pilgrimage of patriotism to the hallowed walls of Fort Sumter, do organize themselves into a permanent Association, to be known as the

"Sumter Club."

ART. 1. The officers of the "Club," shall be the following:

President,
EDWIN R. YALE.

Vice Presidents,
HON. CYRUS P. SMITH, EDGAR KETCHUM.

Executive Committee,
S. M. GRISWOLD, CHARLTON T. LEWIS,
EDWARD CARY.

Secretary,
E. A. STUDWELL.

Treasurer,
RUFUS R. GRAVES.

Chaplain,
REV. T. L. CUYLER.

Musical Director,
WM. B. BRADBURY.

ART. 2. The "Club" shall hold its annual meeting, and elect its officers on the 14th of April, the anniversary of the resurrection of the nation's flag over the walls of Fort Sumter.

Art. 3. Every passenger who left the city of New York, on the steamer "Oceanus," shall be a member of this Club.

Art. 4. All special meetings of the Club, shall be called by the President and Executive Committee.

The following resolutions, reported by Mr. Cuyler, chairman of the committee appointed, were also unanimously adopted:

Resolved, That the cordial thanks of this company be returned to Brig-Gen. Hatch, and Captain Moore, Captain Hunt, and Lieutenant Hagens of his staff, for manifold courtesies extended to us during our visit to Charleston.

Resolved, That to the Neptune Steamship Company, we hereby extend our acknowledgments for the use of their staunch, powerful, and commodious boat, the "Oceanus," and to Captain Young, and the other officers, for their untiring attention to the comfort and pleasure of the party.

Resolved, That we are especially indebted to the Committee of Arrangements, Messrs. Stephen M. Griswold, Edwin A. Studwell, and Edward Cary, for projecting this excursion, and for the entirely satisfactory manner in which they have discharged their varied and arduous responsibilities.

A resolution was also adopted thanking Messrs. Sawyer and Thompson for the piano furnished by them.

Mr. Wm. J. Martin presented to the Sumter Club a Rebel battle-flag, obtained at Charleston, for which he received a vote of thanks.

Mr. Henry C. Bowen moved that the Executive Committee be empowered to arrange for invitation to the meetings of the Club, of the wives of the members who had not been participants in this excursion. This motion was sustained.

Mr. Henry C. Bowen also received a vote of thanks for valuable assistance rendered the Committee of Arrangements.

On motion of Edwin A. Studwell,

Resolved, That a Committee, to be composed of Messrs. James Rice, Geo. E. Brown, and Samuel T. Reese, be appointed to procure a suitable Gold Badge, with the die of Fort Sumter upon it, to designate the members of the Club; said badge not to exceed $5 in cost, and the number not to exceed 150.

The result of a collection taken up for one of the Engineers,* whose foot had been crushed in the machinery, was announced to be $535, and the sum of $80 was subscribed for the Steward. The waiters also were not forgotten, about $30 being raised for them.

Mr. Edwin R. Yale, President of the Sumter Club, cordially invited the members to hold the first meeting at the "Mansion House," of which he is the Proprietor, April 14th, 1866, which invitation was accepted with thankfulness.

Indeed it was remarked that so very thankful a company as ours is very rarely seen.

The Committee appointed to secure some trophy from

*See Appendix.

Charleston, for presentation to the Long Island Historical Society, and the New York Historical Society, reported that they had obtained for this purpose, two 640 pound shots, designed for the Blakely gun, which were acting as ballast on the lower deck. A copy of the Presentation Note to these Societies will be found in the Appendix.

The hour having arrived at which the funeral services had been appointed, coinciding with the hour of the obsequies at Washington, the Rev. Joshua Leavitt, D. D., who presided, introduced the exercises by reading the hymn,

"Through all the changing scenes of life,
In trouble and in joy;
The praises of my God shall still
My heart and tongue employ!"

which was sung to the tune, "St. Ann's," and accompanied by the band.

The Rev. A. P. Graves offered the Opening Prayer.

Rev. Mr. Cuyler then read the 91st Psalm, after which he delivered an address of great pathos, appropriateness, and power, the only report of which appeared in "The Union." We regret that every word could not have been secured, but must be content with publishing all that could be reported by the correspondent of that paper.

Mr. Cuyler began his address by saying:

My Friends and Fellow Countrymen: Grief is as simple as a little child. It seeks no elaborate language; it tolerates no rhetoric; it speaks the plain vernacular, the mother tongue.

We meet to-day as a part of one great mourning family. Beyond the placid waters multitudes of households are mourning, with a grief such as America has not known since Washington died. To-day, a mystic chord, like the electric cable from continent to continent, binds the land in common grief. We cry out "Our father is dead," for in a sense as significant as that of the peculiar people, we may say, "We have Abraham to our Father." We do not mourn him this day as a public magistrate, but as one bound to each of us so subtly, that had we heard this morning that the head of our household had been taken from us, the grief could not have cut more closely; the iron could not have sunk deeper into the heart.

The deed we mourn to day, finds its parallel two hundred years ago, in the assassination of William of Orange, the Deliverer of Holland, who was met on his threshold by the murderer hired by Phillip II. and suddenly stabbed to death. To-day, a despotism more hideous than that of Phillip has aimed an assassin's blow at one whose name shall stand before the centuries with that of William the Silent. I remember standing, a few years since, on the spot where the glorious psalm you have listened to, was read over the remains of John Hampden, the British freeman. With these names, and with that of George Washington, just history will inscribe that of Abraham Lincoln. Not among those whose intellect alone was great; not among the law-givers or the commanders only will we rank our fallen chief, but high above, by the side of that first Father of his Country.

Abraham Lincoln was one of the finest products of American republicanism, and, except Benjamin Franklin, was perhaps, the first great one. He graduated from the common school into the grand college of free labor, whose works were the flat-boat, the farm, the backwoods lawyer's office; and from thence he followed the course of a plain, simple, honest man, true to his God and his country, to his great destiny.

How full of anecdotes and incidents was his precious life. They are as familiar to us as household words. Let me recall one of them, illustrative of his utter simplicity. In 1860, when he visited New York, to make his great speech—intellectually the greatest he ever made before his inauguration—he called with a friend to visit an Illinoian who resided in New York. Entering, he said, "Well, neighbor, how are you getting on in New York?" "I have made," was the answer, "a hundred thousand dollars, and lost it. How have you done?" "Well," said this simple man, "I have worked hard; I have got a two-story house in Springfield, and have laid up some $8,000. They talk some of making me Vice-President with Gov. Seward, and if they do, I can lay up $20,000 out of my salary, and that is as rich as I think any man ought to want to be." And this man was within six months of the highest position on the face of the earth.

Abraham Lincoln was a man of the people throughout. He was open to everybody. I thank God that he was not a man of polished letters, but plain, simple Uncle Abe—Father Abraham. His transparent honesty; how we all know it! He spread his bed in the sun. He laid his whole life open to the day. And his round-about common sense!—did you ever know him to do a foolish thing, to make a foolish speech? It is true he had humor. I am thankful that he was saved from the fearful rasp which his duties would have inflicted on a sterner and colder nature by the good old Christian grace of laughter. And his directness!—remember his words to the Kentucky men: "If slavery is not wrong, nothing is wrong" What cunning sophistries of Calhoun could answer that? Remember, too, these sublime words, freshly uttered: "If God wills that this mighty scourge of war continue until all the wealth piled by the bondsman's two hundred and fifty years of unrequited toil shall be sunk, and until every drop of blood drawn by the lash shall be paid by another drawn with the sword, as was said three thousand years ago, so still it must be said that the judgments of the Lord are true and righteous altogether." That passage will live as long as the English language is spoken.

From this point Mr. Cuyler proceeded with a personal tribute to the loveliness of the President's character, and a description of the manner in which his death must affect the negroes of the South. There was not a dry eye in the audience; every frame was shaken with sobs; a report became impossible.

Mr. Cuyler was followed by Rev. A. P. Putnam, of whose excellent remarks we have no report. He read some extracts from a paper found in Charleston, in which the death of George Washington was announced and commented upon.

Mr. Putnam grew warm with his subject, and spoke with much propriety and feeling.

After singing the hymn,

"How blest the righteous when he dies,"

prayer was offered by Rev. J. Clement French, followed by a brief and feeling address, by Rev. H. M. Gallaher.

The hymn "For a season called to part," was then sung, the band accompanying.

Rev. Mr. Chadwick repeated the Lord's Prayer. The exercises, which had been most solemn and affecting throughout, were closed by singing

America—"My Country 'tis of Thee."

The Benediction was offered by Rev. Mr. Cuyler.

Our good steamer had already brought us within sight of the hills of Nevisink, and we began to gather baggage and relics, to be in readiness to debark. The huge sand heap upon the lower deck, which had been placed there for ballast, and in which had been planted every imaginable variety of the vegetable products of South Carolina, from the timid, blushing rose, and the fragrant mock-orange, to century plants, and sprangly palmetto branches, until the place looked like a young nursery, was now robbed of all these adornments, which were carefully bestowed with the baggage, and all things were made ready for departure from the steamer.

The waters around Sandy Hook were calm as the breast of infancy. The two firmaments of sky and sea, conspired to surround us with the most entrancing beauty. Long Island stretched its low reach of green woodland and Sandy beach, far out of reach to the eastward. The Jersey shore, at the nearer left, retreated in grassy slopes and gently undulating hill-sides. Before us, directly to the northward, stood a large fleet of sloops and schooners, with sails all set, to catch what they might of the scarcely whispering breezes. Do you say it was fancy, when we tell you that at first we exclaimed, "See! even the vessels of the sea are draped in mourning for the Father of the Nation!" For, from every yard-arm in all that fleet, heavy drapery of crape seemed to be depending. The illusion, for a moment, was perfect, but as we neared them, it became apparent that the supposed badges of mourning, were the deep shadows of the yards, thrown downward upon the snowy sails. We changed our relation to the white-winged fleet, and the shadows fled. Not so the shadows from our hearts.

A few moments later, we spoke a British steamer, one of the Cunard line, just out for Liverpool. She announced the "capture of Booth," which caused an exclamation of rejoicing, but papers, soon after received on board, gave no confirmation of the news. That sequel was yet to transpire.

At 3 o'clock we were opposite Coney Island, and looking up the Narrows. At Quarantine, a health-officer boarded our steamer, but detained us only a few moments. The company were standing upon the forward decks, exchanging addresses, extending invitations, calling up reminiscences, protesting enjoyment of the excursion, anticipating re-unions, pointing out objects of interest in either city, and thinking of loving ones, who waited to give them welcome, while the Band, in tones of liquid richness, played "Home, Sweet Home."

The "Oceanus," touched the wharf. Then was there "hurrying to and fro"—adieus were spoken, and many an eye was moist. We emerged from the steamer, into the streets of New York. What a startling change! Ten days before, when we left it, every avenue was a bower of festive, triumphal beauty, ablaze with the brilliant bands, and sparkling stars of the nation's flag; every housetop and mast-head waved them, every spire flung out its variegated welcome to the Dawn of Peace.

Now the metropolis was as mournful as Charleston. Emblems of sorrow, multiplied and funereal as the branches of the cypress, were depending from door-post and balcony, drooping in every window, festooned from cornice and corridor, thickly swathing the lamps along the highways, as for a light extinguished forever; setting in broad frames of black, that brightest and dearest picture, upon which a loyal soul can look, the sunrise colors of the banner; waving solemnly in long black streamers above the starry ensign; speaking eloquently from monuments of symbolic whiteness, in busts and statues of a grand, familiar face and form; in the representations of Columbia's guardian genius, and the Spirit of Liberty, weeping by draped and broken shafts of marble; in the profusion of sadly suggestive tokens, which covered the public courts and halls, and the palatial mansions of the rich, and not less touching and tender in the simple strip of crape, that hung upon the cottage or hovel of the poor. It was the saddest and the sublimest sight which ever met the gaze of any now living man. Yet marvellous as it was, we felt it was but a feeble expression of the sorrow, the chastening, the anguish which reigned within the hearts of the people.

> "Oh pardon us, thou bleeding piece of earth!
> If we are meek and gentle with these butchers!"

But this thought we may not touch.

As all that remained of the honored, loved, and now sainted Lincoln, lay in state in the City Hall of New York, ten thousands of tearful eyes did glance at the pallid, blood-discolored face, pouring all the love of their hearts out in that transient glimpse, while tens of thousands more, wept bitterly that they could not behold, even in death, the features in whose very reflection, they had learned to delight.

Then, in the distant cemetery of his Springfield home, with the voice of prayer, whose pleading he ever invoked, was earth committed to earth, ashes to ashes, and dust to dust. But Patriot—Father—President—Martyr—no far-off tomb can confine him, no rocky sarcophagus can monopolize his dust. There is a shrine for him in every household of the faithful; an earthly home for his omnipresent spirit in every true patriot's heart. They may pile for him in every city, the ever-enduring granite, whose shafts of grey shall defy the corrosion of time, and the lashings of the tempest; they may chisel his form and features in the purest Carrara marble; they may inscribe his name and virtues on stony entablatures, to be set in rotundas of Court and Capital, but his noblest, purest, most indestructible monument is already reared in the memory and affections of every friend of humanity and liberty, throughout the world; in the breast of every patriot freeman, who hails the millennial dawn of the Nation's Redemption; in the heart of every tawny son and daughter, who has ever worn a shackle—and *never*, till the stars shall cease to burn, and the heavens forget to weep, shall their love grow pale, or their tears be dried for *him*, the Deliverer of the Nation, the sent of God. Nor *then*, for we shall meet and know and love him, in the Kingdom of Glory.

For Washington and *thee* twin obelisks shall rise,
Their base the continent—their apex in the skies!

Heaven gives to but one in a century, thine immortality of glory. Thou did'st not know it *here*, but thou art learning its measure there!

Rest and rejoice forever! There can be no more fitting words, with which to close these imperfect records, than the two which need no prefix; which every American will ever be proud to pronounce, and these are,

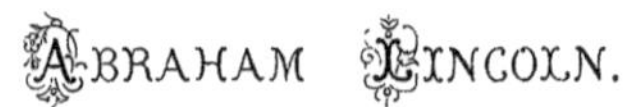

APPENDIX.

Miscellaneous—Documents—Incidents—etc.

COPY OF DISPATCH FROM SECRETARY STANTON TO COLLECTOR DRAPER.

"*Washington, April* 4, 1865.

HON. SIMEON DRAPER :

The steamer Oceanus, chartered by a portion of Mr. Beecher's congregation, has permission to take to the celebration, at Fort Sumter, her complement of passengers, estimated at two hundred or upwards, with privilege of stopping at Hilton Head, Charleston, Sumter, Fort Fisher, Fortress Monroe, City Point, Norfolk, and Portsmouth, to be subject to the customary military regulations at Hilton Head, and other points, and such regulations as may be established by Gen. Gilmore, for the ceremonies at Fort Sumter,

You will please grant the proper clearance.

E. M. STANTON,

Secretary of War.

COPY OF THE PASS ISSUED TO EACH PASSENGER OF THE OCEANUS.

" *Washington, April 1st*, 1865.

HON. SIMEON DRAPER, Collector, New York:

You may permit such vessels as you deem proper, to go to Hilton Head, to witness the ceremonies at Fort Sumter, and carry as passengers such persons as you think properly may go, on the express condition that they report at Hilton Head to Gen. Gillmore, to be subject to his regulations while there.

There should be no privilege of taking passengers indiscriminately, but only such passengers as you may give a special permit. The clearance should be for Hilton Head. The license to go to Charleston to be given only by Gen. Gilmore.

EDWIN M. STANTON, Secretary of War.

COLLECTORS' OFFICE,
NEW YORK, April——1865.

Permit the bearer.................................to embark for Hilton Head, on board of the steamer Oceanus, Capt. Wm. S. Young, in conformity with the above order of the Hon. Secretary of War.

S. DRAPER, Collector.

To WM. S. YOUNG.

This permit to be returned at this office.

COPY OF THE RECEIPT, DULY SIGNED AND STAMPED, GIVEN BY THE PRESIDENT OF THE "NEPTUNE STEAMSHIP COMPANY" TO THE COMMITTEE OF ARRANGEMENTS.

"Received, New York April 8th, 1865, of S. M. Griswold, E. A. Studwell, and Edward Cary, Committee, Eighteen

Thousand dollars, being for passage and fare of one hundred and eighty persons, for a round trip from New York to Charleston, and other points, and thence back to New York, to occupy nine days, to wit: from Monday April 10th, to Wednesday, the 19th, not later than ten o'clock A. M.

For every day thereafter terminating at ten o'clock A. M. the Committee agree to pay Twenty-five Hundred dollars.

$18,000. G. S. HOWLAND, President.

We hereby agree to the above stipulations in behalf of the said 180 persons.

STEPHEN M. GRISWOLD.
EDWIN A. STUDWELL.

COPY OF THE "INSTRUCTIONS TO THE CAPTAIN OF THE OCEANUS," ISSUED BY MR. G. S. HOWLAND, PRESIDENT OF THE "NEPTUNE STEAMSHIP COMPANY."

"NEPTUNE STEAMSHIP COMPANY,"
127 WARREN STREET,
NEW YORK, April 10th, 1865.

Captain Wm. S. Young, of Steamer Oceanus:

DEAR SIR: After receiving your passengers and outfit at Pier 27, North River, on Monday April 10th inst., you will proceed to the port of Charleston. S. C., and thence to such other points as the committee of gentlemen authorized to act on behalf of your passengers may direct; provided you consider the ports or places designated safe for your ship to enter.

You will exercise every precaution to avoid peril by sea, or fire, and every endeavor to promote the safety, comfort, and pleasure of your passengers.

The trip it is contemplated, will occupy nine days, terminating on Wednesday the 19th inst., at or before 10 o'clock A. M. and your owners would prefer that the time be not extended.

You will, however, be subject in this respect to the wishes of your passengers, as expressed through the committee before referred to.

You will request from said Committee timely notice for your departure from place to place, and you will please keep an accurate Journal or Log of all incidents which you may deem important or interesting.

Commending you and your company to Divine protection,

I am, very truly, yours,

G. S. Howland, President.

LIST OF PASSENGERS.

It was proposed on board the "Oceanus," that an autographic list of the passengers should be incorporated within this volume. Subsequently, it was found that this would involve a far greater amount of trouble than was anticipated, and more than would be remunerative to the purchasers of the book. We cannot promise perfect orthographical accuracy. These names are given, mainly as they have been found in the lists already published in Brooklyn and other journals.

"SUMTER CLUB."

President,

EDWIN R. YALE.

Vice Presidents,

CYRUS P. SMITH. EDGAR KETCHUM.

Executive Committee,

S. M. GRISWOLD. CHARLTON T. LEWIS.

EDWARD CARY.

Secretary,

E. A. STUDWELL.

Treasurer,

RUFUS R. GRAVES.

Chaplain,

Rev. THEO. L. CUYLER.

Musical Director,

WM. B. BRADBURY.

S. M. Griswold,
Mr. and Mrs. E. A. Studwell,
M. and Mrs. E J. Ovington,
Mr. and Mrs. James Rice,
Mr. and Mrs. Ed. P. Bray,
J. S. Shultz,
S. L. Husted,
Miss E. Husted,
Edward A. Low,
Rev. A. P. Putnam,
W. F. Gleason,
Edward Cary,
Mrs. D. W. Hinman,
Miss S. A. Duryea,
Miss Phebe B. Merritt,
Samuel T. Keese,
Mr. and Mrs. D. C. Farwell, M. D.
Hon. Alfred M. Wood and Wife,
Mr. and Mrs. George E. Brown,
Wm. Burdon,
Miss E. Colgate,
Norman Hubbard,
Miss Kate Cooley,
" Mary Maghee,
" S. P. Searle,
Mr. and Mrs. Wm. E. Caldwell,
Mr. and Mrs. E. R. Yale,
Mr. and Mrs J. A. Cross,
Wm E. Husted,
Hon. E. A. Lambert,
G. Burchard,
Miss Ianthe Schultz,
Miss Kate Schultz,
Thos. L. Thomell,
H. A. Gouge,
Rev. J. Leavitt, D. D.,
Ed. M. Townsend,
W. Duval,
Henry Seymour,
Stephen S. Hoe,
Richard M. Hoe, Jr.,
A. C. Kellogg.
A. W. Kellogg,
Wm. Arnold,
Wm. Barton,
Rev. H. M. Gallaher,
Curtis Noble,
Mr. and Mrs. Samuel Shethar,
James A. Suydam,
W. P. Vaughn,
David Maydole,
Mr. and Mrs. R. H. McDonald,
Mrs. Weeks,
Geo. C. Robinson,
Samuel Crowell,
Wm. E. Hudson, Jr.
Mr. and Mrs. C. L. Merriam,
Rev. J. J. Chadwick,
E. T. H. Gibson, Jr.
Mrs. C. C. Dike,
Rev. Mr. and Mrs. O. B. Frothingham.
H. C. Reeve,
R. F. Goldsmith,
John Lowe, Jr.
J. F. Hughes,
John Ward, Jr.
R. B. Denny,
Thos. L. Smith,
Jas. T. Atkinson,
John D. Cocks,
Wm. H. Parsons.
J. E. Parsons,

Chas. Taylor,
T. Dwight Martin,
R. S. Guernsey,
H. A. Dike and Niece,
Hon. C. P. Smith,
Miss Ellen L. Smith,
Mr. and Mrs. L. P. Starr,
Mr. and Mrs. D. H. Conkling,
Master Eddie Conkling,
J. A. Perry,
W. A. Perry,
— Colgate,
Mrs. Holmes,
Mrs. Geo. W. Bergen,
Mrs. Geo. H. Roberts,
Mr. and Mrs. A. V. Dike,
Rev. J. C. French,
D. S. Arnold,
Master Arnold,
Mr. and Mrs. Jacob B. Murray,
Mr. and Mrs. A. McCollum,
Mrs. Thos. W. Coughlan,
Thos. H. Maghee,
Mr. and Mrs. Rufus R. Graves,
Mr. and Mrs. Roswell S. Benedict,
L. B. Squiers,
Henry C. Bowen,
Miss Mary L. Bowen,
Miss Grace A. Bowen,
Fred. Ives,
Samuel Stevens,
Mr. and Mrs. B. H. Smith,
Mrs. Edward E. Bowen,
Miss Eliza Cary,
Mrs. Eames,
Mrs. Col. Simpkins,
Rev. Theo. L. Cuyler,
F. H. Richardson,
Chas. H. Marshall, Jr.
Mr. and Mrs. C. T. Lewis,
John W. Minturn,
Rev. A. P. Graves,
Miss Harrison,
Mr. and Mrs. P. A. Dailey,
L. H. Biglow,
F. H. Biglow,
W. M. Aikman,
L. P. Hawes,
Edward Ball,
Charles B. Loomis,
H. H. Crary,
Mr. and Mrs. A. K. Larrabee,
Samuel B. Duryea,
D. R. James,
Dr. Allen and Daughter,
Amos Clark, Jr.,
Rev. J. L. Corning,
Jas. H. Frothingham,
Fred. K. Whitmore,
John J. Cocks,
Aaron M. Powell,
John Stanton,
Wm. H. Lewis,
Orington Lunt,
P. Van Iderstine, Jr.,
W. J. Magie,
Rich'd Howe,
Oliver K. Lapham,
M. F. Lynde,
A. F. Bigelow,
H. H. White,
Wm. Menzies Adams,
Jas. Flynn,
W. A. Spicer,
Mr. and Mrs. Isaac C. Noe,
E. Lewis,
W. E. James,
Oliver Hoyt,
J. L. Leonard,
D. A. Smith,
D. C. Morehead, M. D.,
Wm. W. Dedrick,
E. P. Whittemore,
Aaron Vail,
E. E. Hoffman, M. D.,
Hon. George Hall,
Miss Emma Hall,
Mrs. Hannah F. Voorhies,
Geo. McClure,
Thos. C. Bacon,
J. Corlies White,
Wm. B. Bradbury,
Col. Chas. Howard,
Elias Longley,
Hon. Edgar Ketchum,
Prof. Storrs,
Prof. Gallaudet,
R. P. Corey,
George C. Hall,
Dixon G. Hughes,
Geo. W. Sherley,
Fred'k Wetmore,

Report of the Case of Mr. Swift, the Wounded Engineer.—Operation upon the Foot, by D. G. Farwell, M. D., of Brooklyn.

"On Wednesday morning, tne 12th inst., at about 3.30 A. M., Mr. Swift of Staten Island, who was employed as Assistant Engineer on board the "Oceanus," met with a serious accident from the machinery of the engine—requiring the amputation of his foot. Having provided myself with no instruments for such an emergency, for the excursion, the patient was made as comfortable as possible, until our arrival in Charleston.

At 8 o'clock Friday morning, I procured the assistance of Dr. H. O. Marcy, Surgeon of the 35th U. S. Colored Regiment, who kindly offered the use of his instruments for the occasion. The operation of removing the metatarsal bones from the tarsal, known as Hey's operation, was deemed the most proper one, having in view the necessity of saving as much of the foot as was safe. Complete Anæsthesia by chloform was produced, when the extent of the lasceration of the muscles was ascertained to be more than was at first supposed.

We made a curved incision from the outer portion of the foot, behind the cuboid tarsal towards the phalanges,—thence to the internal cuneiform tarsal, on the dorsal surface, dissecting up the flap so as to admit of the disarticulation of the first metatarsal at its base, from the cuneiform bone, and in turn, the second, third, fourth and fifth metatarsi, from the middle and external cuneiform, and the cuboid bones of the tarsus. The knife was then drawn downward and outward, making a corresponding flap of the plantar portion of the integument.

The arteries being properly secured, (I may here say that a remarkably small amount of blood was lost from the time of the accident, and during the whole operation,) and the flaps approximated, a removal of the head of the cuneiform bone was found necessary, to admit of the union of the flaps.

Sufficient time having been allowed, before closing the wound, to carefully examine the security of the blood-vessels, the sutures and straps were applied, and the stump dressed with cold applications. Twenty minutes was the time occupied in the operation. Anæsthesia soon passing, left the patient in as quiet a condition as could be expected. I ordered a hammock arranged for him, and he returned with the "Oceanus," on the 19th inst.

During the trip, cold water dressings were frequently applied, and the patient is doing well.

Respectfully yours,

D. G. Farwell.

This misfortune of the Engineer, was aggravated by the fact that, just before leaving New York, upon this trip, he had expended nearly all his earnings, in securing exemption from the draft.

The prompt liberality of the passengers, in raising for him a purse of $535, has already been noticed.

Copy of Letter, presenting to the Long Island Historical Society, and the New York Historical Society each, a 640 lb. shot, secured in Charleston.

Brooklyn, May 22d, 1865.

To the Long Island Historical Society:

Gentlemen: At a meeting of the passengers on board the steamer Oceanus, chartered by S. M. Griswold, E. A. Studwell and Edward Cary, Esqs., for the purpose of visiting Charleston, and being present at the flag-raising on Fort Sumter, held on the 14th of April, 1865, the undersigned were appointed a committee to obtain some memorial of the war, to be deposited with the Long Island Historical Society, and the New York Historical Society.

Through the courtesy of General Hatch, commanding at Charleston, and the kindly services of Lieut. John P. L. Weidensaul and Lieut. Collins, the committee were enabled to obtain two 640 pound shots, designed for the Blakely guns (of English manufacture) and which were captured from the rebels on the evacuation of Charleston.

In behalf of the "Sumter Club," an organization composed of the passengers of the Oceanus on the occasion referred to, one of these shots is presented to your Society as a memento of "English neutrality."

Signed,

A. M. Wood,
Edward A. Lambekt,
Cyrus P. Smith,
Committee.

Relics.

Simply to name all the relics which were obtained at Charleston by our company, in their antiquarian researches, would require a volume.

A few only of the most important and interesting can be mentioned.

Mr. Edwin A. Studwell secured the following :

A pass written and signed by James Monroe, while Minister Plenipotentiary at the Court of Great Britain, to Thomas Pinckney, Jr., of South Carolina. As this is a paper of much interest, we transcribe it.

"I, James Monroe, Minister Plenipotentiary of the United States of America at the Court of Great Britain—

"Desire all whom it may concern, to permit Thomas Pinckney, a citizen of the United States of America, to pass without giving or suffering any molestation or hindrance to be given to him ; but, on the contrary, affording him all requisite assistance and protection, as I would do in similar circumstances to all those who might be recommended to me—

"The said Thomas Pinckney is twenty-two years of age, five feet seven inches in height, has grey eyes, dark hair, fair complexion.

"In testimony whereof, I have delivered to him this Passport, dated in London, this 5th day of October, 1803—

JAMES MONROE." seal

This document has a seal of red wax, as large as a fifty cent "shinplaster."

Mr. Studwell also found,

A Treasury paper signed by Alexander Hamilton, while Secretary of the United States Treasury, 1791.

A letter from Lord Fairfax to John Baylis in 1753.

A letter from John Bowden, 1779.

Power of Attorney from Thomas Gadsden.

Power of Attorney from Frederick H. Rutledge.

United States Bank Stock, of ancient date.

Dr. J. Allen brought home as trophies, fragments of the immense Blakely gun, upon the Battery, exploded by the rebels.

Also portions of shell and shot, exhumed from the ruins of Fort Sumter.

Also, books of ancient date from the rubbish of Charleston libraries. The title of one is, "The *Philosophy* of Kidnapping," and contains many passages of curious interest, as a commentary upon the humanity of the "Slave business."

Mr. Edward Ball has on exhibition a number of relics which he secured by much industry—The band from the breech of the Blakely gun—Pair of epaulettes worn by a rebel officer—Fragments from St. Michael's Church—Pieces of shell—Solid shot—and papers of interest.

Mr. Frothingham, of this city, found two or three remarkable letters, written just before the outbreak of the Rebellion, and giving an inside view of the feeling of leading Secessionists.

One gentleman, secured a pair of manacles, which had been in in use in one of the slave-pens.

Another picked up a paper, whose date was lost, purporting to be a copy of enactments passed to regulate the treatment of slaves—providing a fine of £740, for the wilful murder of a slave —£350 for the unintentional murder of a slave, in the ordinary processes of whipping—£70 fine, *for putting out the eye, cutting off the ears, pulling out the tongue*, and *otherwise maiming a slave.*

Fragments of the Submarine Telegraphic Cable, laid between Fort Sumter and Charleston, and the surrounding forts, were brought away, as additional indications of " English Neutrality."

Confederate "Blue-backs," the worthless currency of the Southern States, were bought by the bushel at a merely nominal price, and are now to be seen in any curiosity-shop window, as specimens of very poor engraving, and of an infinitely poorer and now defunct institution.

A MEMENTO OF THE OCEANUS TRIP.

To the Editor of The Union:

Among the many pleasant incidents which occurred during the trip of the passengers of the steamer " Oceanus," to Charleston, at the time of the restoration of the flag on Fort Sumter, was the following, which, if you deem of sufficient interest to present to your readers, you will please insert in " The Union :"

Mrs. B., who was making observations in her own peculiar way, having strayed a little from the party accompanying her, was accosted by a black woman, with a hen under one arm and a basket of eggs under the other, saying, " Missus I want to give the Northern ladies something, but I have nothing but this hen and these eggs; will you please take them ?" The kindness of heart shown by this poor woman, was too much for the sympathetic nature of Mrs. B.; but what to do with the hen and its products, so far from home, was a question not easily settled. A compromise was soon agreed to; the eggs were taken, and the hen left. A "souvenir" was put in the woman's hand, and she departed in much delight. She soon returned, however, with more eggs, which were received by another Mrs. B., and a "deposit" made, as above, in the hands of the woman.

In discussing the question on the homeward passage, what should be done with the eggs, our friend Mr. W. E. C.—who is ever on the alert "to do good as he has opportunity"—proposed to the ladies, to take the eggs up to his country seat, and put them under the care of the most motherly hen in his large flock. This arrangement was carried out, and a letter just received from my friend C., gives the result:

ARMENIA, N. Y., June 10, 1865.

DEAR SIR:—I am happy to inform you that the Charleston hen has done her duty, as well as could be expected under the circumstances.

The eggs were evidently the product of secession times, and stoutly resisted all Northern influences.

But the mother-hen determined, "*a la* Gen. Grant," to set it out on this nest "if it took all summer." A great destruction of capital has been the result, but "victory at last" has rewarded her efforts, and she is now followed by a train of four bipeds, one black, one white, and two octoroons.

I have neglected to tell you that the mother-hen is black, and struts with pompous pride above her white and octoroon subjects.

They will be cherished and nourished with care, and if they escape all the ills incident to chicken childhood, they shall be present at the inauguration of the Sumter Sociable next winter.

Mrs. C. and myself unite in much regard to Mrs. B. and yourself.

Respectfully yours,

W. E. C.

"Victory at Last!!"

How appropriate that this popular, truthful and spirited glee, should conclude these pages! Victory—honor—peace—glory—at last!

Mr. Bradbury has very kindly furnished us the stereotyped plate of the song, as it was daily sung by all the passengers during the memorable trip of the "Oceanus."

VICTORY AT LAST.

SONG AND CHORUS.

Words by Mrs. M. A. Kidder *Music by* Wm. B. Bradbury.

2. The heroes who have gained it,
   And lived to see that day,
We will meet with flying banners
   And honors on the way;
And all their sad privations
   Shall to the winds be cast,
For all the boys are coming home—
   There's victory at last.—*Chorus.*

3. O happy wives and children,
   Light up your hearts and homes,
For see, with martial music
   "The conquering hero comes,"
With flags and streamers flying,
   While drums are beating fast;
For all the boys are coming home—
   There's victory at last.—*Chorus.*

From the "Golden Censer," *by permission.*

www.ingramcontent.com/pod-product-compliance
Lightning Source LLC
LaVergne TN
LVHW011229110826
845150LV00006B/1586

9781425515089